HOLLYWOOD URBAN LEGENDS

The **TRUTH** Behind All Those Delightfully Persistent **MYTHS** of **FILM**, **TELEVISION**, and **MUSIC**

RICHARD ROEPER

NEW PAGE BOOKS
A division of The Career Press, Inc.
Franklin Lakes, NJ

HOLLYWOOD URBAN LEGENDS
Edited, designed, and typeset by Stacey A. Farkas
Cover design by Cheryl Finbow
Printed in the U.S.A. by Book-mart Press

To order this title, please call toll-free 1-800-CAREER-1 (NJ and Canada: 201-848-0310) to order using VISA or MasterCard, or for further information on books from Career Press.

The Career Press, Inc., 3 Tice Road, PO Box 687, Franklin Lakes, NJ 07417

www.careerpress.com
www.newpagebooks.com

Library of Congress Cataloging-in-Publication Data

Roeper, Richard.
    Hollywood urban legends : the truth behind all those delightfully persistent myths of film, television, and music / by Richard Roeper.
        p. cm.
    Includes index.
    ISBN 1-56414-554-9 (hc.)
    1. Motion pictures—United States—Anecdotes. 2. Television broadcasting—United States—Anecdotes. 3. Urban folklore—United States. I. Title.

PN1994.9 .R58 2001
791.4'0973—dc21   2001030565

Acknowledgments

Julia Roberts rambled on for more than four minutes in her acceptance speech at the 73rd annual Academy Awards, and yet she didn't thank anybody connected with this book. Julia, you've changed.

But that's okay, I'll do it myself.

First, my family: Robert and Margaret Roeper, Nick and Lynn Zona, Bob and Colleen Roeper, Laura Roeper, Sam Saunders, Laura Renee LeQuesne, John LeQuesne, Emily Roeper, Caroline Roeper, and Bobby Roeper.

Thanks and love to Bill Adee and Joyce Winnecke, and to Grace Adee. Also, Leslie Baldacci, Michelle Carney, Michael Cavoto, Jacqueline Colbert, Michael Cooke, John Cruickshank, CarrieAnn DeYoung, Roger Ebert, Robert Feder, Carrie Francis, Michael Gillis, Sherri Gilman, Drew Hayes, Hank the Angry Drunken Dwarf, Jocko Hedblade, Mary Kellogg, Anita Huslin, Pam Klein, Rick Kogan, Bebe Lerner, David Radler, Phil Rosenthal, Neil Steinberg, Jenniffer Weigel, Nigel Wade, Jim Wiser, Bill Zehme, Bill Zwecker, the terrific staff of *Ebert & Roeper and the Movies* and the wonderful publicity team at Buena Vista Television.

The lifetime achievement award goes to my agent, Sheree Bykofsky.

Kudos to the gang at Career Press: Ron Fry, Anne Brooks, Jackie Michaels. Special thanks to my editor, Stacey Farkas.

This book could not have happened without the tireless efforts and creative input of my research associate, editor-for-life and movie-loving sidekick, Paige Smoron. She is the American Bridget Jones and then some.

And finally, I'd like to thank the Internet, for making urban legends more popular than ever before.

Contents

INTRODUCTION 9

TV

Back to *The Fugitive* 13
Joanie Loves What? 21
"And the Password Is..." 24
Touched by an Atheist 28
Myths of the Super Bowl 32
"Willy Gilligan" and the Seven Deadly Sins 39
Arnold on a Spit 43
Cosby Buys *The Little Rascals* 45
Bert and Ernie Are Gay and Dead! 48
The Newlywed Game Blooper 54

PAST LIVES

Mel Gibson: Man Without a Face? 63
Bogart the Gerber Baby? 68
Did the Duke Dodge the Draft? 73
Cher's Rib Removal 80

Hanoi Jane Fonda 84

Marilyn's Dress Size 89

MOVIES

Fargo-ing the Truth 95

Briefcase Full of Soul 99

Johnny Rocco's Recount 104

I'm Drunk and You're a Prostitute 108

The Jesus Chronicles 113

Casa-bunka 119

The Curse of *Poltergeist* 123

FACT OR FICTION?

Tom Green's Nazi Prank 129

Monica Puts Foot in Mouth 134

Johnny Carson's Quips 138

"Lido Deck, Sir?" 143

Unrelated Legends 146

Was Lucy a Commie? 151

Mean Martha Stewart 158

The Celebrity Snub 162

MUSIC

Madonna, Tip-Top Starlet 169

Let It Bleed 174

It's Not Easy Being a Green CD 178

Eminem Lives! 183

"Fire and Rain" 187

"The Little Girl" 191

Blondie Blunts Bundy? 196
Puffy Dragon 200

LEGENDARY DEATHS

Mama Cass and the Ham Sandwich............................207
Code *Blue's Clues* 212
The Curse of James Dean 216
Death of the Marlboro Man...221
Dead Legends.. 227

AND FINALLY...

Women Speak in Estrogen... 237

BIBLIOGRAPHY AND NOTES 241

INDEX 253
ABOUT THE AUTHOR... 256

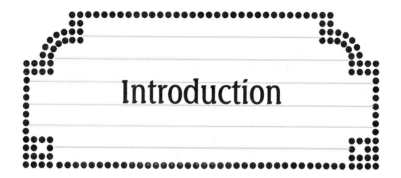

Introduction

It's the first rule of celebrity life: The moment you become famous is the moment when people start telling lies about you.

Ninety-nine percent of these rumormongers will never meet you, never have a conversation with you, never be wronged by you, never have any reason to spread untruths about you—but that won't matter. What matters is, you belong to the world, and the world is filled with people who love to spread salacious tales about people in the public eye, whether those stories have any basis in fact or not. After all, you're not a flesh-and-blood human being with feelings; you're a celebrity, and this is part of the trade-off. If you didn't want to be the target of such stories, why didn't you stay in your hometown and find work as a forklift operator or a receptionist?

That's the rationalization used by "civilians" who revel in bogus stories about celebs. If you don't like it, remove yourself from the roster of the famous.

The power of rumor and innuendo is so widespread that you're probably familiar with at least half of the 50 or so celebrity-based urban legends (ULs) recounted in this book. Perhaps you've even participated in the continuation of a UL's life by repeating the "true stories" about *The Newlywed Game* blooper, or Humphrey Bogart and the Gerber baby, or that tasteless prank that MTV's Tom Green played at a Bar Mitzvah. Not that I'm condemning you for such behavior; after all, I've done it myself (see "The Celebrity Snub" on page 162). But as I tried to do with my first book on this topic, *Urban Legends*, I'm once again attempting to throw a little light on some murky myths and outright lies, this time concentrating on stories about movie stars, pop music icons, TV shows, and former child actors who aren't dead, no matter what you might have heard.

Adam Rich is alive and well. Mama Cass didn't choke on a ham sandwich. And "Puff the Magic Dragon" is actually about...well, see for yourself.

—*Richard Roeper*
February, 2001

Back to
The Fugitive

*D*EAR STACY: *Please settle a bet. Wasn't* The Fugitive *series based on the classic novel* Les Misérables?*—Mitch R., New York*

DEAR MITCH: *Actually, the 1960s TV series was inspired by the story of Sam Sheppard, the Cleveland dentist convicted of murdering his wife. Sheppard, who died penniless in 1970, spent 10 years in prison before the U.S. Supreme Court overturned his conviction in 1966. He always insisted that a "bushy-haired intruder" killed his wife and knocked him unconscious after a struggle on the night of July 4, 1954....*(Chattanooga Times, *August 1, 2000)*

First off, let me say that I love the idea of someone named "Mitch R." in New York making a bet about such literary matters, rather than the usual Mets-against-Yankees stuff. I can just picture the scene as Mitch and his friend—let's call him Vinnie—are on a loading dock somewhere on Long Island, as Mitch flips through the newspaper.

MITCH: "It says here there's going to be a new TV series based on *The Fugitive*, this time starring Timothy Daly of *Wings* fame."

VINNIE: "Is that so? Well, it will be difficult for Daly to match the angst of David Janssen's performance in the original series, or the intensity Harrison Ford displayed in the big-screen adaptation. But I do enjoy his work."

MITCH: "Well, the key is the material. And with *The Fugitive* based on Victor Hugo's classic novel, *Les Misérables*, I don't see how it can be a bad program."

VINNIE: "What have you been smoking? In *Les Misérables*, Inspector Javert was the bad guy, and the hunted one, Jean Valjean, was the good guy."

MITCH: "Yes, but in both cases, the hunted man does good deeds."

VINNIE: "But everyone knows *The Fugitive* was based on the Sam Sheppard case!"

MITCH: "Was not!"

VINNIE: "Was so!"

MITCH: "Not!"

VINNIE: "I'll bet you a hundred bucks!"

MITCH: "You're on! There's only one way to settle this: I'll write my letter to Stacy right now!"

Not that Stacy was advancing any new theories with her assertion that *The Fugitive* TV show of the 1960s and the subsequent revival movie and television series were based on the sensational case of Dr. Sam Sheppard. (By the way, Stacy:

Sheppard was an osteopathic physician specializing in surgery in the Cleveland suburb of Bay Village, not a dentist.) For nearly 40 years, ever since *The Fugitive* premiered on ABC-TV in 1963, it's been an accepted part of pop culture lore that the story of the wrongly convicted Dr. Richard Kimble and his single-minded pursuit of his wife's killer was inspired by the circumstances of the Sheppard case.

Before O.J. Simpson came along and didn't kill Nicole Brown Simpson and Ronald Goldman, many observers considered Sheppard to be the "star" of the most sensational trial of the last half of the 20th century.

Some background: Dr. Sam Sheppard was a successful physician who, by outward appearances, seemed to be living the American dream of the 1950s. In addition to his thriving career, his personal life was seemingly idyllic. He had married his high school sweetheart, Marilyn, and they had a fine son and a lovely home on Lake Erie in a posh suburb of Cleveland.

But the dream was shattered on the night of July 4, 1954, when Marilyn Sheppard was bludgeoned and attacked in her bed while the Sheppards' 7-year-old son slept in a room down the hall. Sam Sheppard claimed that he had fallen asleep downstairs and was awakened by his wife's cries for help; he said he stumbled through the dark house, up the stairs and into the bedroom, where he encountered a "bushy-haired stranger" who knocked him unconscious. When Sheppard awoke, he saw his wife's bloody body. (It was later determined that she had been struck as many as 35 times about the face and head with a blunt instrument.) After ascertaining that his wife was deceased and checking to make sure his son was all right, Sheppard said he heard a noise on the first floor and ran downstairs. He saw a "form" running outside and followed it to the shore of Lake Erie, where he once again lost consciousness. When Sheppard regained consciousness, he had only a hazy memory of what had happened. He returned to his home, called Bay Village Mayor Spencer Houk (who was a family friend) and said, "My

God, Spence, get over here quick. I think they have killed Marilyn."

But police and prosecutors didn't buy Sheppard's "intruder" story, and on July 30, 1954, he was arrested and charged with his wife's murder. After several weeks of intense publicity, the Sheppard case went to trial on October 18, 1954. During the proceedings it was revealed that Dr. Sheppard had maintained a "swinging" lifestyle and had carried on with a car dealer's wife and a lab technician, and that he and Marilyn had had a volatile relationship.

Two months later, a jury convicted Sheppard, and he spent 10 years in prison before the Supreme Court overturned the verdict, ruling that overwhelmingly prejudicial pretrial publicity had tainted the first verdict.

In 1966, Sheppard was tried again, this time for second-degree murder. He was defended by flamboyant attorney F. Lee Bailey and was acquitted.

Sheppard died broke in 1970, still thought of as guilty by millions, yet still maintaining his innocence. In the spring of 2000, the Sheppards' son, Sam Reese Sheppard, went to court with a wrongful imprisonment lawsuit that he hoped would clear his father's name once and for all. Sam Reese's attorneys tried to use DNA evidence to make the case that a third person's blood was found at the scene—but the passage of time had left them with less-than-perfect specimens, and after 10 weeks of testimony from more than 70 individuals, the eight-person jury took less than six hours to reject Sheppard's claim. In November of 2000, an attorney for Sheppard argued that the jury was too swift in its deliberations and the ruling should be overturned or a new trial ordered.

And when the Associated Press reported this latest development, the story said: "The civil trial...was the latest episode in the sensational murder case that inspired the movie and TV series *The Fugitive*."

Or did it? In the summer of 2000, as CBS started promoting a new version of *The Fugitive*, with the aforementioned Tim Daly as Dr. Richard Kimble, Mykelti Williamson as the dogged Lt. Philip Gerard, and Stephen Lang as "the one-armed man," the man who created the franchise told reporters that *The Fugitive* is not now and never has been based on the Sheppard case.

Roy Huggins, now in his mid-80s, is the creator and/or executive producer of such TV shows as *77 Sunset Strip*, *Maverick*, *The Virginian*, *Baretta*, *The Rockford Files*—and *The Fugitive*. In the summer of 2000, Huggins, along with the stars of *The Fugitive* and executive producer Arnold Kopelson, met with TV critics from across the country. At a press conference, Huggins explained the genesis of *The Fugitive*:

"I've never gone independently out there to say [*The Fugitive*] is not based on the Sheppard case. But constantly I'm asked if it was. The answer is no. I was writing and directing movies [here in Hollywood] when the murder took place. It was 1954. And I didn't even know about it.

"In 1960, I came up with *The Fugitive* and I had *The Fugitive* concept all in order, except for one thing: What did he do for a living before he got into this terrible mess? And I thought it over and decided that, one, at that time anyway, everybody liked doctors. And two, if I made him a doctor, that meant that we could increase the suspense immeasurably on occasion. When here he is dressed like a plumber and someone gets badly hurt and he has to exercise his skills and his obligations as a doctor to do something that no one can believe this plumber is doing. And he is, in effect, exposing himself.

"So that's why he became a doctor. It was a year later that F. Lee Bailey took over the case and it got more publicity, but that was long after I had already made Dr. Kimble a doctor."

Actually, Huggins has often made the rather curious claim that he hadn't even heard of the first Sheppard trial when he created the concept for *The Fugitive* several years later.

"I invented *The Fugitive* in 1960, and I had never heard of Sam Sheppard," Huggins told the *Pittsburgh Post-Gazette* in a story published in February of 2000. "I don't care whether people say *The Fugitive* was based on the Sheppard case. The only reason I deny it is it happens to be the truth."

At least Huggins is consistent with his denials. In 1993, as the movie version with Harrison Ford was racking up big numbers at the box office, Huggins was telling essentially the same tale: "I suppose connecting Kimble to Sheppard makes a more sensational story," Huggins told the *Los Angeles Times* in 1993. "I wouldn't care as much, except that's not the way *The Fugitive* happened. The news reports are in reckless disregard of the truth."

And in Ed Robertson's book *The Fugitive,* published that same year, Huggins again denies the Sheppard connection.

But Sheppard's son, Sam Reese Sheppard, isn't swayed by these multiple denials. In an interview for this book, Sheppard said: "I respect my elders, but [Huggins] is speaking Hollywood legalese. He's speaking the language of Hollywood, which is, deny everything so you don't get sued. The man must have been living in Siberia [not to have heard of the case]. It was the [O.J.] Simpson case of its day. It was the print media abuse of the century....

"The first script [for *The Fugitive*] called for 'the red-haired man,' and in the Sheppard case, it was the bushy-haired stranger."

But Sheppard (who believes a window washer is the true murderer of his mother) has written a book called *Mockery of Justice* about the case and acknowledges that the success of the original *Fugitive* series was beneficial to his father's defense.

"*The Fugitive* connection did keep the Sheppard case alive. It was a double-edged sword. My dad was in prison, we were exhausted financially and emotionally. You need to have a notorious case, or the money to keep it going. F. Lee Bailey has been quoted widely as saying that the connection was there—that's how the American public knew about [our case].

"It's just disappointing that these people can't own up and be honest about it...In all honesty, they should step up to the plate, admit it, and pay a little bit for where the story came from.

"I can say this, [the story] is an American legend now. I try and respect that. It's very disappointing that people don't realize that, step up and be responsible about American history here."

Let's take a look at the similar threads running between the two stories:

★ Dr. Sam Sheppard, wrongly convicted of his wife's murder. Dr. Richard Kimble, wrongly convicted of his wife's murder.

★ Sheppard said the real killer was a "bushy-haired intruder." Kimble, at least in the version we all know, maintained that the real killer was a "one-armed stranger."

★ Marilyn Sheppard was pregnant when she was murdered. In a flashback episode of *The Fugitive*, we learned that the character of Helen Kimble had been pregnant, but the child had been still-born a short time before the murder.

★ Dr. Richard Kimble escapes from a train wreck and has a series of adventures while staying one step ahead of Gerard (and one step behind the one-armed man), whereas in the real world, Dr. Sam Sheppard never escaped and never brought the real killer, if there is such a person, to justice.

In the end, it comes down to motive. If Roy Huggins had used the Sheppard case as the basis for *The Fugitive*, nobody would have accused him of doing anything wrong, as countless plays, novels, and scripts have been inspired by actual events. If anything, he would have been praised for recognizing the dramatic potential of the real story and transforming it into an episodic gem. Huggins has no motive for denying the connection, and because he is the only one who truly knows what was in his mind's eye when he first envisioned *The Fugitive* some 40 years ago, we should take him at his word and categorize the Sheppard–Kimble connection as urban legend.

Joanie
Loves What?

Scott Baio: superstar.

You say BAY-oh, I say BUY-oh, but however you pronounce his last name, Scott Baio is one of the most impressive men in the history of show business. Not because of the work he has done on such lame sitcoms as *Joanie Loves Chachi* and *Charles in Charge,* and in bad movies like *Zapped!*, but because Baio has been able to date practically every beautiful buxom blonde starlet in Hollywood during the last 20 years, despite having had such a consistently mediocre career.

A partial list of Baio's reported lovers includes Pamela Anderson, Nicole Eggert, Heather Locklear, Denise Richards, even his *Chachi* co-star Erin Moran, and "most of the girls on *Baywatch*," in the words of Willie Aames, the curly-haired doofus who was the cut-rate Jerry Lewis to Baio's Dean Martin. The now 40-ish Baio has also dated an endless string of supermodels, models, and almost-models.

How does he do it? Is he a master hypnotist? Perhaps the truth is this simple: He's a handsome, talented, wealthy, considerate man who would be a perfect companion for any saline-enhanced gal who comes to Hollywood with dreams of making it big.

Either that or *there is no God.*

Most sitcom heartthrobs fade into dinner theater obscurity after a couple of years (where have you gone, Joey Lawrence?), but if anything, the Baio legend has only grown with time. Late-night comics David Letterman and Conan O'Brien often invoke the Baio name in monologues and routines, and the still-magnetic actor occasionally drops in on Howard Stern's show to talk about his latest projects and conquests.

Maybe it's all about the Chachi. People just love the Chachi thing. The character first appeared on *Happy Days*, with a teenage Baio playing Chachi Arcola, a skinny little greaser who worshipped his Uncle Fonzie, and had a thing for the rapidly developing Joanie Cunningham, played by Erin Moran. The young characters were so popular that in March of 1982, they were given their own spin-off series, *Joanie Loves Chachi*, which had a run of just 17 original episodes spaced out over an 18-month period, but still lives on in the hearts and minds of some very sad people, most of whom are institutionalized or in their late 30s and still living with their parents. (Believe it or not, there's actually a *Joanie Loves Chachi* Web site, an elaborately designed page that includes a detailed episode guide and news about all the actors who appeared on the show. Not long ago, the guy who played Bingo even posted a grateful e-mail to fans. How did he find the time?) In the spin-off, Joanie and Chachi moved to Chicago and started robbing banks and holding up liquor stores—ah, just kidding. They moved to Chicago with Chachi's mother and his new stepfather, Al, to pursue singing careers. *Joanie Loves Chachi* scored strong ratings in the spring of 1982, but it was steamrolled by *The A-Team* that fall, and was removed from the ABC-TV schedule the following spring.

But there was one last moment of glory for the show, courtesy of worldwide syndication. When *Joanie Loves Chachi* premiered in Korea, the first episode was the highest-rated program in that country's history.

Was it Baio's mysterious magic at work again? In a way, yes, because his character's name sounds almost exactly the same as the Korean word *chaji*.

And *chaji* means *penis*. So millions of Koreans tuned in for a show that they thought was called *Joanie Loves Penis.*

This tale thrives on dozens of sitcom-related Web sites, and Baio, as well as *Happy Days* co-creator Garry Marshall, has told versions of the story in interviews—though Marshall has sometimes said the country in question is Thailand, not Korea.

It is true that the word *chaji* means *penis* in Korean. A spokesman for a Korean Web site told me, "In response to your rather strange question, one of the [Korean] words for *penis* is *cha-jee*, with emphasis on the first syllable." But *Joanie Loves Chachi* has never run on any Korean TV station and thus has never been measured by any ratings service in that country. The program was broadcast on the Armed Forces Korean Network, but it was played in English, for American audiences. The story that *Chachi* reigned in Korea is pure urban legend.

Scott Baio's love life, however, remains an unexplained mystery far more astounding than any urban legend.

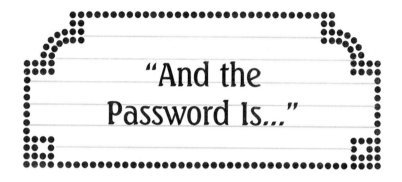

"And the Password Is..."

This urban legend is usually ascribed to the old *Password* show, though I've also heard it associated with the *$25,000 Pyramid*. In either case, the particulars are pretty much the same: A Caucasian celebrity (Alan Alda, Tom Selleck, Charles Nelson Reilly, and Jack Klugman are among those who have "starred" in this UL) has a partner who is black and is not particularly well educated or articulate.

At a key moment in the game, the secret word is "deer," so the celebrity says the word "doe" as a clue. It's the obvious choice: Doe, a deer, a female deer....

So the celeb says, "doe," and his partner hesitates for only a moment before the lightbulb goes on and he says, "knob!"

Get it? "Doe—knob"? Remember, the contestant in this story is a not-so-bright black man. According to ugly stereotype, he would pronounce "door" as "doe," which is how he comes up with the non sequitur of "knob."

According to the legend, the audience falls apart, as does the host and the celebrity player. It's such a humiliating moment for the black man that he runs off the show, disgraced beyond belief. He gets his revenge, however, when he files a lawsuit against the show and its syndicate, who decide to settle out of court for a large sum of money rather than subject themselves to a highly publicized trial.

Right. As if a jury would award a plaintiff millions because he embarrassed himself on national television. If that's all it took, imagine how many made-for-TV idiots would be clogging the courtrooms!

This UL contains a not-so-hidden agenda: to perpetuate a stereotype. Whereas most ULs are equal-opportunity stories enjoyed and shared by people of all races, I've never heard this one told by anyone who isn't white. Maybe that's because a lot of blacks wouldn't find it all that funny.

This story isn't quite as ubiquitous as *The Newlywed Game* blooper (see page 54), but there's no shortage of people who swear they saw the "doe-knob" moment on TV. Game show staple Jamie Farr has even convinced himself he was there when it happened, as he recounts in his unforgettable autobiography, *Just Farr Fun*:

An all-time favorite Super Password *show happened on the watch of host Bert Convy. I was in a bonus round that had escalated to an all-time high of $50,000. My partner was a black woman who had won her way into this bonus round with me. We were both pretty keyed up. After all, a $50,000 prize on this show was very rare.*

So now we begin. Behind her, I could see a list of 10 words. Behind me, she could see a series of letters. My job: to feed her 10 rapid-fire clues that would trigger in her the right 10 words, all in 60 seconds. If the first word was "daughter," I might say, "Son?"

...So, I look up and see the first word on our list is "deer." She sees, behind me, the letter D. *Now I could have said, "animal." But if I wanted to be more specific, I might have said, "antelope?" Instead, quick-like, I say, "Doe." I was thinking of that song in* The Sound of Music. *But she comes back, just as quick, with, "Knob."*

I blink. "Doe...knob"? Well, aside from the fact that "knob" doesn't begin with a D, I didn't say "door," I said "doe." But she heard "door." I couldn't go on. I just started to laugh so hard that Convy had to restrain me. The audience was dying. The only one who didn't know what was happening was the contestant. But Convy and I had to compose ourselves, and just try to go on. Needless to say, we didn't win the $50,000....

Hope you enjoyed that rare and fascinating glimpse into the storytelling genius that is Mr. Jamie Farr. I still can't believe *Just Farr Fun* wasn't nominated for a National Book Award. Maybe they should have entered it in the fiction category.

The problem with Farr's story is this: *Super Password* with Bert Convy made its debut in late September, 1984. Farr didn't appear on the show for the first time until December of 1984. That story had already been in circulation for years before Farr's appearance. In fact, a *Sports Illustrated* article earlier that very year recounted the story, with Nipsey Russell as the *Password* celebrity contestant who uttered the "knob" response. (If anyone tells you they saw something like this happen on the *$25,000 Pyramid*, it doesn't compute. The object of that game was to match words with categories, so if someone said, "doe," you wouldn't say "deer" or even "knob," you'd say something like "female animals.")

Beyond all that, the story as it's always told defies logic. For the sake of argument, let's say someone's dialect is such that when he says the word "door," it sounds like "doe" to many ears. That doesn't mean that he's hearing the word as "doe," it just means he doesn't clearly articulate the *r* at the end of the word. So if someone else says the word "doe," it doesn't sound like "door" to him, it sounds like "doe."

Follow me? For the urban myth to even work within the constraints of the stereotype, it should be the black man who says "door" as "doe." That would then lead to the white celebrity saying, "knob."

Think about it.

Touched by an Atheist

Famous atheist Madalyn Murray O'Hair is such a pest. Even when she's dead, she's trying to get religious-themed programming off the air! I know it's true because I received an e-mail detailing all the particulars, and we all know that e-mails are *never* misleading, right? Here's what it said:

Madeline Murray O'Hare [sic], an atheist, whose efforts successfully eliminated the use of Bible reading and prayer from public schools 15 years ago [sic], has now been granted a federal hearing in Washington, D.C., on the same subject, by the Federal Communications Commission. Her petition, No. 2493, would ultimately pave the way to stop any reading of the Gospel of our Lord and Savior, Jesus Christ, on the airwaves of America. She has a petition with more than 287,000 signatures....

Another widely circulated e-mail about O'Hair's crusade mentions a popular program that will be forced from the airwaves should she succeed:

CBS will be forced to discontinue Touched by an Angel *for using the word "God" in every program. Madeline Murray O'Hare's* [sic] *organization has been granted a federal hearing on this subject by the Federal Communications Commission. Her organization's petition, No. 2493, would ultimately pave the way to stop the reading of the Gospel of our Lord and Savior on the airwaves in America. They've got 287,000 signatures! This group is also campaigning to remove all Christmas programs and Christmas carols from public schools!*

You can help! We are praying for at least one million signatures. This could defeat their effort and show that there are many Christians alive, well, and concerned about our country. We must unite on this. Please don't take this lightly. We ignored this lady once and lost prayer in our school and across the nation. Please stand up for your religious freedom and let your voice be heard. Please forward this message to everyone you know....

First of all, if Madalyn Murray O'Hair shows up in the year 2001 for a federal hearing, I'll bet she denounces her past and proclaims her belief in God, what with the fact that she'd be coming back from the great beyond and all.

O'Hair and her son and granddaughter disappeared from San Antonio, Texas, in August, 1995, along with $500,000 in gold coins. She was presumed dead. Former O'Hair colleague David Waters was scheduled to go on trial on five federal counts alleging that he and others kidnapped O'Hair and her family and killed them. His case wasn't helped any when, in February of 2001, the remains of four people were found in a shallow grave on a ranch in south Texas. In March of 2001, the remains were positively identified as O'Hair's. Investigators said they believe O'Hair, her son, and granddaughter were murdered, dismembered at a public storage shed in Austin, placed in

55-gallon drums, and then buried on the ranch in 1995. (The skeletal remains of a fourth and as yet unidentified body—a male—were also discovered in the shallow grave.)

Even if O'Hair were to miraculously return to earth as a spirit bearing a placard saying, "Whoops, I Was Wrong!" the one thing we know she hasn't been doing is leading a campaign to have *Touched by an Angel* removed from the airwaves because of its constant references to God. The petition cited in the e-mails was the work of two broadcasters who, in 1974, tried to get the Federal Communications Commission to ban religious organizations from getting licenses to do business on noncommercial educational channels. (It was titled petition RM-2493.) The FCC refused to consider the petition, citing First Amendment rights. O'Hair wasn't even involved in that aborted crusade, yet her name has been attached to the phantom campaign to get *Touched* booted. The fact that O'Hair's first and last names are almost always spelled wrong and that she's been missing since the mid-1990s hasn't made much of an impact on the thousands of people who apparently believe that their favorite feel-good show is truly in danger. (Also, O'Hair's infamous lawsuit to have "The Lord's Prayer" banned from her son's school reached the United States Supreme Court nearly 40 years ago, not the 15 years ago cited in the e-mail.) The rumor that O'Hair was spearheading an antireligious broadcasting drive has ebbed and flowed over the years, with the FCC fielding thousands of calls and receiving thousands of petitions with literally millions of signatures—all of them unnecessary. They're protesting something that never happened—and is not happening now.

Things got so crazy that in the early 1980s, the FCC asked Congress for $250,000 in funds to counter the petitions with a mass mailing campaign of its own, explaining that there wasn't anything out there to protest in the first place! These days the FCC's Web site has a release about the urban legend, titled, "Religious Broadcasting Rumor Denied." It reads, in part: "A rumor has been circulating since 1975 that Madalyn Murray O'Hair, a widely known, self-proclaimed atheist, proposed that the Federal Communications Commission (FCC) consider limiting or banning religious programming. This rumor is not true. A petition filed in December 1974 by Jeremy D. Lansman and Lorenzo W. Milam [that] was routinely assigned the number RM-2493 added further confusion regarding the issue of religious programming. They had asked, among other things, that the FCC inquire into operating practices of stations licensed to religious organizations...The 'Lansman-Milam petition' was rejected by the FCC on August 1, 1975...Periodically since 1975, the FCC has received mail indicating that, in many parts of the country, there were rumors claiming the petitions of RM-2493 had called for an end to religious programs on radio and television. Such rumors are false. Since 1975 to the present time, the FCC has received and responded to millions of inquiries about these rumors. Many efforts have been made by the FCC to advise the public of their falsehood."

A spokesman for the FCC told me, "I'd be happy to deny [the rumor] categorically. It's the same rumor; they've just added on this *Touched by an Angel* thing. It's just the latest version of [something] that's been going on for 25 years now, and we can't seem to shut it down."

The FCC does not have, nor does it seek, the authority to prevent TV stations from showing programs with a religious theme. After all, how many religious-themed mini-series and specials, not to mention broadcasts of movies like *Ben-Hur* and *The Robe* and *Jesus Christ Superstar*, have been shown over the years? If the FCC ever did have such frightening clout and an inclination to wield it, *Touched by an Angel* wouldn't be the only program threatened. The only way Roma Downey and friends will be sent packing is if the Nielsen gods no longer smile upon them.

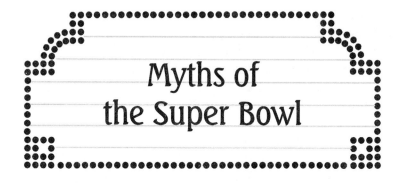

Myths of
the Super Bowl

Super Bowl Sunday is not an official American holiday,
but it might as well be, given that approximately half the
country's population observes and participates in such rituals
as Super Bowl Week, Super Bowl wagering, Super Bowl office
pools, and of course Super Bowl vegging out on the day itself.

More adults watch the Super Bowl than participate in the
electoral process. Some people even decorate their homes or
paint their faces in the colors of their favorite teams. Those
people are known as "losers."

As a nation, we pay more attention to Super Bowl Sunday than we do to real national holidays such as Presidents'
Day, Martin Luther King Day, even (sadly) Veterans' Day. On
those aforementioned weekday holidays, our main concerns
are if we have to go to school or work, if there will be mail

delivery, and whether or not we have to feed the parking meters. Let's be honest, it's not as if 100 million Americans gather around the family TV sets on Presidents' Day to watch nine hours of television about Washington and Lincoln. Our priorities are more askew than Charles Grodin's toupee in a tropical storm.

Given the enormous magnitude of the Super Bowl, it's not surprising that a whole roster of urban legends has sprung forth regarding the game. You'll hear and read these same stories year in and year out, repeated by the news media and by football fans as gospel truth—but now you'll know better, because you're reading this.

Following are the most enduring Super Bowl myths.

WATER PRESSURE DROPS AND SEWAGE SYSTEMS ARE OFTEN BROKEN BECAUSE TENS OF MILLIONS OF VIEWERS GO TO THE BATHROOM AT HALFTIME AND FLUSH THE TOILET AT THE SAME TIME.

First of all, it's more likely that the typical Super Bowl viewer will go to the bathroom during the game, rather than miss one of those million-dollar commercials or the Super Bowl halftime show, which has become such a lavish spectacular that it would have made Liberace blush. The idea that people would rather go to the bathroom than watch something like the 2001 spectacle that featured Steven Tyler and Britney Spears singing a duet on "Walk This Way" is crazy. Who would want to miss those swiveling hips, that flowing hair, the heavy makeup, the elaborate costume, the sexually charged persona (not to mention Britney!)?

Stories about water mains breaking after big-event TV shows have been around ever since The Beatles played on *The Ed Sullivan Show*. Such disasters also supposedly occurred after the first moonwalk, during breaks in the Academy Awards shows, and after the final episodes of *M*A*S*H*, *Cheers*, *Seinfeld,* and *The Michael Richards Show*. (Just kidding about that last one.) It is true that flow-meter increases in water usage can be attributed to the ending of an enormously popular event programming, but that doesn't mean pipes will start bursting and floods will occur, as systems are equipped to handle such fluctuations. (In Atlanta, for example, the water lines are built to handle up to four times the average water flow, and the Super Bowl creates about double the average.)

As for the Super Bowl, the incident usually cited as "proof" is the 1984 breaking of a water main in Salt Lake City, Utah—which really did happen. But by all indications, it was just a coincidence that it occurred on Super Bowl Sunday. (A city official's joking remark to a radio reporter that the main probably broke because of the Super Bowl is the probable ignition point of this UL.) As a public utilities official for Salt Lake City told the *Los Angeles Times*, there was no link established between the Super Bowl telecast and the break of the 16″ pipe. The truth is that because much of the infrastructure of the city is old and worn, water-line breaks have been all too common.

The water-level legend received an unintended credibility boost during the week leading up to Super Bowl XXI, when the commissioner of the New York City Department of the Environmental Protection Agency issued a facetious statement urging fans hosting parties to encourage their guests to make bathroom trips in staggered fashion rather than in clusters in order to keep the water pressure level relatively stable. It was supposed to be a joke, but many people took it seriously. When are people going to learn that if you mess around with urban legends, they'll come back and bite you like a rabid wolverine?

★ ★ ★

You can predict the stock market based on
the winner of the Super Bowl.

The theory works like this: If a team from the old American Football League wins, the market will be down; but if a team from the old NFL (and that includes a few AFC teams who have switched conferences) is victorious, it'll be a bull market. The 2001 Super Bowl was won by the Baltimore Ravens, an AFC team that used to be the Cleveland Browns. So that means it's an old NFL team that won and so 2001 should be a good year. In the 34 Super Bowl years prior to that, the correlation proved correct 28 times—or 82 percent of the time.

All right, but so what? If you spend enough time matching annual records of World Series wins or Stanley Cup victories with the performance of the stock market, you are eventually going to find some random pattern that can be manipulated into an eyebrow-raising "statistic." (And note also that in 1998 and 1999, the Denver Broncos won the Super Bowl, which should have been an ominous sign—yet those were two boom years for the market.) Unless Alan Greenspan suits up for the game, there's obviously no cause-and-effect between the outcome of a championship football game and the performance of the stock market for an entire year—and if you believe otherwise, I've got some shares in the Statue of Liberty I'd like to sell you.

DOMESTIC VIOLENCE AGAINST WOMEN INCREASES
DRAMATICALLY ON SUPER BOWL SUNDAY.

The volatile mix of so many testosterone-charged men drinking and gambling while watching a violent game on TV would seem to be a recipe for domestic violence, so it's easy to understand why so many people have fallen for this myth. The supposed link between Super Bowl Sunday and domestic violence was first established in the public eye during Super Bowl Week of 1993, when a coalition of women's and antiviolence groups held a press conference and told reporters that an Old Dominion University study had found that "40 percent more women will be battered on Super Bowl Sunday than [on] any other day," making it "the biggest day of the year for violence against women."

That same week, an author and psychologist went on *Good Morning America* with basically the same claim, and a number of columnists and media commentators repeated the assertions as fact. Well-intentioned NBC-TV even ran a public service announcement about violence against women that ran during the game, in effect forfeiting precious seconds of advertising time in the name of a greater cause.

Enter the skeptics. Ken Ringle of *The Washington Post* actually tried to find the study in question, which supposedly had been conducted three years prior to the press conference. The professor who conducted the survey told *The Post* that it wasn't about the Super Bowl specifically; and what she did find was that there was no definitive correlation between Washington Redskins football games on TV and reports of domestic violence against women in the region where those games were shown. It was later revealed that one of the spokespersons at the press conference knew that her colleague was misrepresenting the survey, but she chose not to correct her in front of the media.

Although the Super Bowl Sunday–domestic violence myth is repeated every year, there's no data to back the claim.

"Certainly violence occurs on [Super Bowl] Sunday as it does on other Sundays," Rita Smith of the National Coalition Against Domestic Violence told *USA Today* in a January, 2001, interview. "But we can't look at the Super Bowl as the cause of domestic violence because that doesn't explain why women are battered on May 15 or any other day."

SUPER BOWL SUNDAY IS A GREAT DAY TO TAKE THE FAMILY TO A DISNEY THEME PARK, BECAUSE THEY'RE PRACTICALLY EMPTY!

Simply not true. To put things in perspective, let's take a look at the ratings for Super Bowl XXXV. Because the Baltimore Ravens and the New York Giants were defense-oriented teams without a lot of marquee appeal and the game turned out to be a rout, the numbers were low for a Super Bowl—but still astronomic compared to "regular" TV: a 40.3 rating and a 60 share. That means an average of 40 percent of the nation's TV homes were watching, and 60 percent of all TVs in use were tuned to the game. According to CBS, about 130 million people watched at least part of the game.

But hold on. That means that 60 percent of the nation's TV homes were not watching the Super Bowl, and more than half the country's population didn't tune in for a single minute. More than 150 million people did something else on Super Bowl Sunday, and that includes a healthy number of folks who went to Disneyland or Walt Disney World.

The least popular month at Disney theme parks is actually February, in the weeks just after the Super Bowl.

TWO-THIRDS OF ALL AVOCADOS SOLD ARE PURCHASED WITHIN A WEEK OF THE SUPER BOWL, AS PARTY HOSTS PREPARE MOUNTAINS OF GUACAMOLE DIP.

It's more like 5 percent. And according to the California Avocado Commission, the most popular day for avocado sales isn't Super Bowl Sunday but...Cinco de Mayo!

OF ALL THE RIDICULOUS QUESTIONS ASKED BY THE MEDIA DURING SUPER BOWL WEEK, THE WORST WAS WHEN A SPORTSWRITER ASKED DOUG WILLIAMS OF THE WASHINGTON REDSKINS, "HOW LONG HAVE YOU BEEN A BLACK QUARTERBACK?"

Stories about the hype and hoopla surrounding the Super Bowl inevitably include this anecdote about Super Bowl XXII—for example, ESPN's Chris Berman telling it to his viewers in January, 2000. But the truth is that the question was never asked.

The media were constantly asking Williams about being black, and Butch John, a reporter with the *Jackson* (Miss.) *Clarion-Ledger* who had covered Williams at Grambling State University, was mocking the situation when he said, "Doug, it's obvious you've been a black quarterback all your life. When did it start to matter?"

In an article that ran in the *Atlanta Journal-Constitution* in January, 2000, John said, "Everybody got a pretty good laugh out of it. His answer was that it didn't matter until he got to the NFL. That answer was used in the wire services. Also, there was a little blurb—no more than a paragraph—in the San Diego paper the next day, about 'A question from a well-meaning writer.' From there, things just kind of shot out of control. By the end of the week, it was the question."

"It's not embarrassing," John added. "It just bothers me that someone would take something fifth-, sixth-, seventh-hand, and turn it into something else. It's like one of those urban legends."

Exactly.

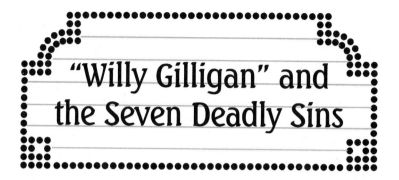

"Willy Gilligan" and the Seven Deadly Sins

What a group of misfit castaways they truly were, from the fat guy who always thought he was in charge to the old crank to the sexy young babes to the unathletic guy who couldn't do anything right.

No, I'm not talking about the first season of *Survivor,* I'm talking about *Gilligan's Island*.

Now, you might think of *G.I.* (as Tina Louise has always insisted on calling it in interviews because she can't bear to say the name "Gilligan" any more) as nothing more than an astoundingly idiotic, stupid sitcom with no redeeming values—a brainless exercise in lamebrained humor that will play forever in Rerun Hell.

Well, you're probably right. But there are those who believe that *Gilligan's Island* is so much more complex than that.

★ 39 ★

The show's creator, Sherwood Schwartz, is a learned and so-phisticated man who always felt guilty about going into television, because he knew his creative genius could have been put to better use in another field, like rocket science or plastics. Deep down, Schwartz wanted to give the world TV programs that would educate us, that would tell us something about the human condition, that would elevate the human spirit—but the powers-that-be at the network level didn't want to hear that sort of nonsense. They wanted funny hits—commercially viable pap that could be used to sell dishwashing detergent and new cars to the masses.

In other words, they wanted *Gilligan's Island*.

Little did the execs at CBS know that Schwartz played a trick of sorts with *Gilligan's Island* by giving it a subliminal second life that existed as a running social commentary about the state of the world. Not even the writers or cast members knew about this, but the truth is, they each represented one of the seven deadly sins!

1. Ginger, with her Marilyn Monroe voice and her plunging-neckline gowns, was Lust.

2. Mary Ann, who could never be as sexy as Ginger, was Envy.

3. The Professor, who could construct a telescope from a coconut shell and bragged about knowing a little bit about everything, was Pride.

4. Mr. Howell, the millionaire, was Greed.

5. Mrs. Howell, who treated the other castaways like they were her servants and never did anything herself, was Sloth.

6. The Skipper, with his insatiable appetite, was Gluttony.

and

7. He was also Anger, for constantly losing his temper and hitting Gilligan with his hat.

And that leaves the deceptively benign Gilligan, who was Satan himself. *Gilligan's Island* is actually Hell! He keeps the others there through one foul-up after another. Week after week, the castaways are allowed to glimpse a ray of hope that they'll be able to get off the island, but it's all a mirage. They never realize that they're doomed to spend all eternity there—courtesy of Gilligan, who always wears red, the most devilish of colors.

Gilligan's Island as a metaphor for Hell is also Schwartz's way of admitting his own existence was hellish. Just as the castaways were trapped on that island, Schwartz was trapped in the mindless world of TV sitcoms, doomed to spend his professional life wallowing in shallow inanity.

Pretty deep lagoon we're wading in, eh? Academic journals and Internet philosophers have delighted in advancing the "Seven Deadly Sins" theory of *Gilligan's Island*, and in later years, Schwartz himself has not discouraged such thought.

Whether the castaways really represented the seven deadly sins is almost too loony a concept to contemplate—but there are other *Gilligan* issues that trouble me. What I want to know is, why did those people pack overnight luggage for a "three-hour tour"? And why the hell didn't the Professor, Skipper, or Gilligan ever make a serious move on Ginger or Mary Ann? You say these men were marooned, I say they were in paradise! Ginger and Mary Ann were fantabulous babes. You had three single men and two attractive young gals on that island; somebody should have been posting a sign on their door saying, "If the hut's a rockin', don't bother knockin'."

Over the last decade or so, Hollywood has been churning out one movie after another that's been based on a Boomer TV series: *The Addams Family; Car 54, Where Are You?; Lost in Space; The Fugitive; Wild, Wild West; Maverick; The Flintstones; Sgt. Bilko; Charlie's Angels*, and so on. Never mind that most of these movies are unwatchable; the studios keep making them because it's easier than coming up with fresh ideas. If they ever do a big-screen adaptation of *Gilligan's Island* (Adam Sandler as Gilligan, Penelope Cruz as Mary Ann, Paul Newman and Joanne Woodward in campy cameos as the Howells), I hope they at least have the sense to make it an R-rated romp that finally addresses the reality of what would happen if people were stranded on an uncharted desert isle for years on end.

As for the title character's name, there are some Gilliganiacs who claim his full name is Willy Gilligan, and that this information is contained either in a "lost" pilot episode or in the first regular season episode.

It is true that CBS never aired the first pilot for *Gilligan's Island*, as it contained a number of actors who didn't make the final cut for the show. And in the first episode, aired on September 26, 1964, a radio broadcaster lists many of the castaways by their full names, including Jonas Grumby (the Skipper), Roy Hinkley (the Professor), Ginger Grant, and Mary Ann Summers. (The Howells were identified as Mr. and Mrs. Thurston Howell, though Lovey's actual name was revealed to be Eunice in a subsequent episode.)

But Gilligan was just...Gilligan. And the name "Willy" was never invoked for the run of the series. Schwartz is quoted in Bob Denver's autobiography as saying that the character was named Willy Gilligan in the "original presentation," whatever that means—but in his own book about the show, he never addresses this world-shaking issue. All I know is, I'm glad the name didn't catch on with young parents in the mid-1960s, or there would be a bunch of 35-year-old men named Gilligan walking this Earth right now.

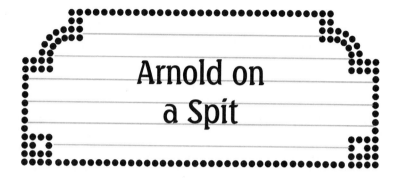

Arnold on
a Spit

Of all the idiotic comedies of the 1960s, from *Gomer Pyle, U.S.M.C.* to *My Mother the Car* to *The Beverly Hillbillies*, perhaps the most lame-brained of all was *Green Acres*, which starred Eddie Albert and Eva Gabor as two wealthy city-dwellers who shuck it all to go live on a farm. I think they explained why in the opening theme song, but I could never get through the whole song, because the entire premise was beyond ridiculous—even for a kid watching reruns after school. *Green Acres* was so bad, I almost preferred doing homework or cleaning up my room.

Probably the biggest star on the show was the charming pig, Arnold Ziffel. Fans of *Green Acres* tell me that Arnold was always stealing scenes from Eva Gabor—which might be the only act of thievery that's actually easier than taking candy from a baby. According to TV lore, Albert (an admittedly fine character actor) and Gabor weren't exactly big fans of the pig, and during the last season, they plotted their revenge.

Arnold was dead meat, so to speak.

After the final show was filmed, Albert and Gabor held a big barbecue on the set for all of the cast and crew. And right there in the center of the party, roasting on a spit, was Arnold Ziffel himself. Some of the crew thought it was a cruel trick, and they voiced their feelings before leaving the party in disgust. But others were glad to see Arnold where he belonged, and they sat down for a hearty meal. Snort, snort.

Ah, come on. In reality, there was no one pig who played Arnold Ziffel. During the complete run of the series, as many as a dozen pigs were used. (What, like somebody was going to be able to tell the difference? If Lassies can be interchangeable, certainly multiple Arnold Ziffels wouldn't be a problem.) One pig pretty much looks like another. According to Frank Inn, who worked as a trainer on the show, when *Green Acres* was canceled, the pigs were sent to farms where they were allowed to live peacefully. There was no Arnold-munching cast party.

Nor did the cast of *Babe* eat the star pig after the original movie or its sequel, contrary to popular rumor. That's just an update on the Arnold Ziffel story.

Cosby Buys
The Little Rascals

In the 1970s, *The Little Rascals* series was as popular on the after-school and weekend rerun circuit as *Three Stooges* shorts and old episodes of *Gilligan's Island*, *The Andy Griffith Show,* and *Hogan's Heroes.* Some of my friends were so familiar with the mini-movies starring "the Rascals" (or, as they were originally known, "Our Gang") that they could identify the plots within 30 seconds.

Not me. I just never got into the grainy, crackly, old black-and-white movies about a bunch of urchins who talked like they had marbles in their mouths. Give me an innuendo-laced episode of *Love, American Style* any day!

But there's no denying the legacy of *The Little Rascals.* From the early 1920s through the mid-1940s, the legendary Hal Roach—a mentor to Laurel and Hardy and Abbott and

Costello and the producer of classic early TV series such as *The Lone Ranger*, *Blondie*, and *Topper*—produced more than 220 featurettes about the adventures of kids with nicknames like Spanky, Alfalfa, Chubby, and of course, Buckwheat, and those stories lived on for years via television syndication. (By the way, Eddie Murphy's famous impersonation notwithstanding, it was Porky, and not Buckwheat, who had the signature phrase, "Otay!")

Nowadays, though, you'd be hard-pressed to find a single major television station in the country that carries *The Little Rascals*. Nor has it become part of the campy rotation on cable's TV Land and Nick at Nite. Even if you have digital TV, DirecTV, a satellite dish, and four remote controls, you probably couldn't find an episode of *The Little Rascals* on a bet.

That's because they're gone forever. Years ago, Bill Cosby paid several million dollars for the rights to all 220-plus of *The Little Rascals* mini-movies—just so he could destroy the original prints and prohibit the broadcast or sale of any *Rascals* material in any form.

Or so the urban legend goes.

Anyone familiar with Cosby's life and career knows that he has always been a champion for positive black images in the media. Not only has Cosby been a trailblazing example through his roles in *I Spy* (the first dramatic series to co-star an African-American man), *Cosby*, and *The Bill Cosby Show*, but he has contributed millions of dollars to African-American colleges, and he once produced and narrated a documentary about negative portrayals of African-Americans in the media.

It would stand to reason, then, that Cosby might not be the biggest fan of *The Little Rascals*. Even though the series showed young black and white children playing together, most of the characters were broad stereotypes, and many jokes were downright racist. Buckwheat might have been a lovable kid as well as great comedic fodder for a young Eddie Murphy on

Saturday Night Live, but his name has become a derogatory term that no one would ever use in 2001—unless you were deliberately trying to insult somebody. (Hal Roach had a reputation for being a decent, racially enlightened person, but it's worth noting that he also brought the horrid spectacle that was *Amos 'n' Andy* to television.) Many years ago, when King World Syndicate acquired the rights to *The Little Rascals*, representatives of the NAACP were asked to assist with the editing of several of the film shorts so that the most egregiously racist gags about eating watermelon, etc., could be eliminated. And some episodes, including "Lazy Days," "Moan & Groan, Inc.," "Little Daddy," and "A Tough Winter" (which co-starred Stepin Fetchit), were dropped from the rotation entirely.

However, it is not true that Cosby subsequently purchased the rights to the *Rascals* just so he could retire them permanently. (A similar UL has Ted Turner so offended by the way *The Dukes of Hazzard* portrays Southerners as ignorant rednecks that he buys the rights to the show just so he can mothball it.) In fact, *Little Rascals* video collections are readily available in many stores and on the Internet; as of this writing, there were more than 40 *Little Rascals* tapes, as well as a *Best of Buckwheat!* compilation for sale on the Web. (A few years ago, a company named Cabin Fever Entertainment released the entire collection of *Little Rascals* comedies as a 21-volume set. When Hallmark bought the company, though, the series was discontinued.)

It just may be that you're not seeing *The Little Rascals* in regular syndication because the material is too old, too dated, and, on occasion, too politically incorrect for the 21st century.

I, for one, don't miss them.

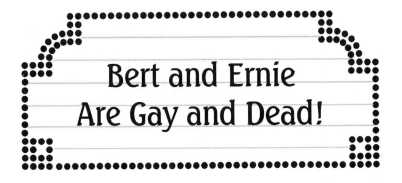

Bert and Ernie
Are Gay and Dead!

Sometimes *Sesame Street* intersects with an entire subdivision of urban legends. Consider the stories that have been attached to just one Muppet:

★ Ernie is named after a character from *It's a Wonderful Life*.

★ Ernie is gay.

★ Ernie has AIDS.

★ Ernie is dying of leukemia.

★ Ernie was killed in a car crash.

★ Ernie is dead.

For a harmless fuzz puppet whose only function has been to entertain the kiddies on the most beloved children's show in the history of television, Ernie has quite a track record!

Often his pal Bert comes along for the ride, as in the oft-repeated factoid that the two Muppets were named after characters from *It's a Wonderful Life*.

You'll recall that in the town of Bedford Falls, Ernie the cab driver and Bert the cop were friends of George Bailey's, and they serenaded Bailey and Mary on their wedding night. Character actor Frank Faylen, who played Ernie, also had roles in *The Lost Weekend* and *Funny Girl*, and he played Herbert T. Gillis, Dobie's dad, on the TV series *The Many Lives of Dobie Gillis*. Ward Bond, who played Bert, was a stellar supporting presence in more than 200 films including *Mister Roberts* and *Rio Bravo*, and a TV star in the 1950s with *Wagon Train*. But for holiday audiences in the 21st century, Faylen and Bond will forever be linked by the relatively small roles they have in *It's a Wonderful Life*—and younger viewers will inevitably laugh the first time they hear Jimmy Stewart's character make reference to "Bert and Ernie." Hey, just like the Muppets!

Trivia books and newspaper articles have often made the claim that Jim Henson was a big fan of *It's a Wonderful Life*, and thus he named his Muppet characters after the cabbie and the cop from the movie.

"The characters Bert and Ernie of *Sesame Street* were named after Bert the cop and Ernie the taxi driver in Frank Capra's *It's a Wonderful Life*," asserted Natasha Weale in the February 20, 1999, edition of the *Scottish Daily Record*.

"Creator Jim Henson was a big fan of the movie," explained the *Detroit News* in an article in 1996.

"Jim Henson was a fan of *It's a Wonderful Life*," said the *Dallas Morning News* in a 1992 article on the subject.

And so it goes.

The great Jim Henson died in 1990, and as far as I could ascertain, there's no public record of him ever commenting on the *It's a Wonderful Life* connection. However, there's a solid file of circumstantial evidence that works against the theory.

First, there's the timeline issue. It's possible that Henson loved Capra's movie—but at the time when Bert and Ernie were hatched in the 1960s, *It's a Wonderful Life* was a 15-year-old movie that had performed poorly at the box office in its initial release and was out of circulation. The movie became a holiday perennial only after TV stations began showing it nearly round the clock for three weeks every December, year after year. (Because the film was in the public domain, TV stations were able to show it as many times as they wanted to, at no cost; however, the copyright now belongs to NBC, which has exclusive rights to the film.) So Henson would have been tapping a relatively obscure film for inspiration if he had indeed named his Muppets after a couple of minor characters.

In the January 3, 2000, edition of the *San Francisco Chronicle*, longtime *Sesame Street* writer Jerry Juhl weighed in on the rumor with a letter to reporter Jon Carroll: "I was the head writer for *The Muppets* for 36 years and one of the original writers on *Sesame Street*. The rumor about *It's a Wonderful Life* has persisted over the years…I was not present at the naming, but I was always positive it was incorrect. Despite his many talents, Jim had no memory for details like this. He knew the movie, of course, but would never have remembered the cop and the cab driver…."

Juhl goes on to recount a conversation he had with the late Jon Stone, the first producer on *Sesame Street*, who told Juhl that "Ernie and Bert were named one day when he and Jim were studying the prototype puppets. They decided that one of them looked like an Ernie, and the other one looked like a Bert. The movie character names are purely coincidental."

Henson's death in 1990 led to the creation of another urban legend: the imminent demise of Ernie. The man who voiced Ernie was gone, and this planted the seed for rumors that the Muppet himself would be laid to rest.

In a 1991 letter to the editor of the *New Hampshire Sunday News*, college student Michael Tabor protested the impending death of Ernie: "Their plan is to slowly deteriorate Ernie by giving the viewing audience the impression that he has leukemia, eventually killing him." Tabor launched a petition drive to save the character and collected hundreds of signatures—and anyone who signed the petition no doubt passed on the story to a handful of friends, who told their friends, and so on, and so on.

The details of the story shifted from region to region. Sometimes it was reported that Ernie had died in a car crash; other times it was said that he had AIDS. Occasionally it was Bert, and not Ernie, who was dancing with the Grim Reaper.

Rarely, if ever, did anyone point out that we were talking about a PUPPET. It's my duty to point out that puppets might get a little ratty with time, but they don't even age, let alone die.

"I wish I could say how many illnesses we've heard and calls we've had," said a spokesman for the Children's Television Workshop in a 1993 interview in the *Louisville Courier-Journal*. "Unfortunately, we're hearing a lot of rumors, everything from that he's got leukemia to the story that he was hit by a bus.

"Ernie is alive and well and we have no intention of anything happening to him or anyone else."

In fact, Ernie had a great resurgence in the late 1990s, as Sleep 'n' Snore Ernie became the hot gift item. (Note that it was Sleep 'n' Snore Ernie, not Sleepin' Corpse Ernie.)

Not that *Sesame Street* hasn't tackled the reality of mortality. In 1982, Will "Mr. Hooper" Lee died, and rather than just write him off the show by having him move to another street, the creative team came up with an episode in which Big Bird learns that Mr. Hooper is gone and won't be coming back. It was groundbreaking television.

Perhaps the fact that *Sesame Street* had previously dealt with this issue gave further credence to the notion that Ernie was going to be killed off. It's one thing to say a tender good-bye to a man and the gentle character he played, but quite another to arbitrarily bump off a Muppet. What were they going to do, have poor Ernie's hair falling out as he lost weight and became disoriented? Have Bert and the gang all attend a memorial service for their fallen Muppet comrade?

As a spokesman for the show told the *Baltimore Sun* in 1997: "*Sesame Street* is a children's show. We certainly wouldn't kill off one of our Muppets."

Bert and Ernie have also had to contend with rumors about their personal lives. Just how "close" are those two close buddies (wink-wink)?

This UL has its origins in a satirical work penned by Kurt Anderson in 1980 called *The Real Thing*. (Anderson's later projects would include *Spy* magazine and the media-oriented Web site Inside.com.) Addressing rumors about the sexual orientation of celebrities, Anderson mentioned the two Muppets: "Bert and Ernie conduct themselves in the same loving, discreet way that millions of gay men, women, and hand puppets do. They do their jobs well and live a splendidly settled life together in an impeccably decorated cabinet."

Amazingly, some people took Anderson's obviously glib comments to be a statement of fact about Bert and Ernie, and the rumor mill started churning. In 1993, *TV Guide* received batches of letters from readers railing against *Sesame Street* for condoning a homosexual relationship, and in 1994, a North Carolina preacher began a campaign on his radio show to have Bert and Ernie banned from *Sesame Street*. Around the same time, there were rumors that the touring production of *Sesame Street Live* was to include a skit where Bert and Ernie got married!

Right.

Watch any episode of *Sesame Street* and you'll notice that it's more about learning to count than exploring the sexual urges of oddly charming puppet characters—with the exception, of course, of Miss Piggy's stalkerish zest for Kermit the Frog. (Interesting that people have never been freaked out about a possible pig–frog union, but the concept of homosexual Muppets is seen as a sign of the coming apocalypse.) Bert and Ernie are a couple of simple-faced creatures with an *Odd Couple* friendship; nothing more, nothing less.

As the Children's Television Workshop said in a press release circa 1993:

> *Bert and Ernie, who've been on* Sesame Street *for 25 years, do not portray a gay couple, and there are no plans for them to do so in the future. They are puppets, not humans. Like all the Muppets created for* Sesame Street, *they were designed to help educate preschoolers. Bert and Ernie are characters who help demonstrate to children that despite their differences, they can be good friends.*

It's a wonderful life, isn't it?

The Newlywed Game Blooper

L ong before there was a Jerry Springer or a Sally Jesse Raphael, there was a Bob Eubanks, a man who oozed slick charm as he presided over a daily circus of intimate and embarrassing revelations from just-married couples who were willing to humiliate themselves on national TV in order to win refrigerators and lawn mowers.

It was called *The Newlywed Game*.

But unlike other bright and brassy and loud game shows of the era—like *The Match Game* and *Beat the Clock* and *Joker's Wild*—*The Newlywed Game* wasn't just a game show, it was the *Who Wants to Be a Millionaire* of its time. Created in 1966 as a standard daytime offering, *Newlywed* was so popular that a prime-time version was quickly added and ran from 1967 to 1971. And even after the prime-time edition was canceled, the daytime version continued on until 1974, and there have been two successful revivals of the format and title since then.

Its chief appeal was sexual. The smarmy, leering, plastic-haired, California-tanned Eubanks, who looked and talked like the kind of guy who would try to have an affair with one of the dewey-eyed young brides on the show, would quiz four couples to determine which pair had the closest relationship. Husbands were asked to predict how their wives would answer a series of questions, and vice versa. Usually the questions had to do with sex, for example, "When your husband makes love to you, which jungle animal does he most resemble?" But nobody really cared who won. The show's signature trademark was its 1960s-era, naughty-snicker titillation quality. What everyone remembers are the moments when the wife would hit the husband over the head with his answer card as he stammered to explain why he had said that her little sister had the best body in a bikini he'd ever seen.

One exchange, in particular, lives on as perhaps the most oft-quoted game show moment in television history. I speak, of course, of the time when a young woman uttered the immortal phrase, "In the butt, Bob!"

It went something like this. The husbands were squirreled away in a soundproof room while Eubanks asked the wives his typically invasive questions about their personal lives.

With a wink and a smirk at the camera, Eubanks said, "Ladies, where will your husband say was the most unusual place you've ever made whoopee?"

When the studio audience's laughter died down, Contestant Number One blushed and said something like, "In my parents' bedroom while I was supposed to be babysitting."

Contestant Number Two's response was something along the lines of, "At the drive-in theater during a showing of *Bambi*."

And then it was time for Contestant Number Three. Eubanks repeated the question—"Where's the most unusual place you've made whoopee?"—and she didn't even hesitate before replying, "That would be in the butt, Bob."

It brought the house down, of course. Eubanks tossed his index cards into the air and doubled over with laughter, the studio audience howled, and even the other young wives were in hysterics. At first, the poor gal who'd blurted out the graphically honest answer didn't understand why everyone was laughing so much—but as she replayed the moment in her mind, she realized she'd misinterpreted the question, to say the least. Mortified, she hid her face in embarrassment and stammered an apology.

After a commercial break, the husbands were back on the set and of course everyone was eagerly awaiting the "most unusual place" question. The husband of Contestant Number Three went with, "In the park," at which point his wife sheepishly held up the cue card reading "IN THE BUTT," as Eubanks deadpanned, "Sorry, but your wife had a slightly different response."

"God damnit, I was going to say that!" said the husband, and the place went up for grabs once again.

For years I've heard variations on this story from people who swear they were watching when the exchange took place, and for years I've assured them that it never happened, that they were victims of a mass case of manufactured memory. (Even though *The Newlywed Game* thrived on innuendo and often employed a "cuckoo-cuckoo" sound effect to bleep over forbidden words, it's hard to imagine a reference to anal sex getting on the air, even with several words bleeped out, back in the late 1960s or early 1970s. Seems more likely they would have scrapped the question altogether or re-taped that particular segment.) You hear a story so many times that you convince yourself that not only did it really happen, but you remember it happening.

It's such a famous tale that when *Playboy* interviewed Pamela Anderson in February 1999, the interviewer said: "As Bob Eubanks would ask, what's the strangest place you've ever made whoopee?" and Anderson replied, "That'd be in the butt, Bob!"

You've got to love a chesty pepperpot who knows her urban legends.

Eubanks himself has said it's a figment of group imagination. He has half-jokingly offered a $10,000 reward to anyone who can produce irrefutable evidence of the segment's existence, and he's even had T-shirts printed up saying, "It Never Happened!" because he's tired of talking about it every day of his life.

"It never happened," he told *Entertainment Weekly* magazine in a 1997 interview. "No matter where I go, it's mentioned three or four times a day. [But everybody] swears they saw it."

The *EW* interviewer persisted: "But did you ever ask the question, 'Where's the weirdest place you've made whoopee?'"

Eubanks replied, "Oh yeah. It's one of my all-time favorite questions."

On one level, Eubanks seems to have it right. No one has ever been able to produce a clip or even an audiotape of the "most unusual place" question and answer exactly as it has been told and retold millions of times.

But a funny thing happened to this story on the way to Urban Legend Land. Turns out that it contains more than a couple of grains of truth—and in this case, the Internet has served as a conduit for accuracy instead of a launching pad for the spread of misinformation.

Here's the deal. If you log on to *www.hitplay.com*, you'll be able to watch and hear a RealPlayer clip of a *Newlywed Game* show from 1977, during one of the aforementioned revivals of the show. The clip is said to be from a Game Show Network rebroadcast of the program (can you *believe* there's a cable channel devoted to reruns of game shows?), and it appears to be legitimate, with neither sound nor picture doctored. Eubanks had asked the husbands "the strangest place you've ever had the urge to make whoopee," and a guy named Hank had said, "The freeway."

The clip begins after the wives have rejoined their husbands. Hank's wife is named Olga, and what follows is a transcript of the dialogue.

> EUBANKS: "Here's the last of our five-point questions. Girls, tell me where, specifically, is the weirdest place that you personally, girls, have ever gotten the urge to make whoopee. The weirdest place...Olga?"
>
> OLGA: "Ummm..."
>
> EUBANKS: "Yes, Olga?"
>
> OLGA: "Uh..."
>
> OLGA'S HUSBAND HENRY: "Go ahead."
>
> EUBANKS: "Yes, Olga."
>
> OLGA: "I'm trying to think. Ummm...Gee Henry, what did you say?"
>
> EUBANKS: "Hey, don't ask him. He can't help you out at all!"
>
> OLGA: "Is it ——"
>
> *(NOTE: Here Olga's words are bleeped out with the familiar "Cuckoo!" sound effect. Some UL detectives on the Internet swear she says, "in the ass," but I've watched the clip a dozen times and find it impossible to decipher. In any case, the studio audience erupted in laughter, as did Olga's husband and the host of the show....)*

EUBANKS: "No, no, no, no. No, what I'm talking about
is the weirdest location, the weirdest place...."

OLGA: "The weirdest location. I don't know."

Obviously Olga, wherever she is today, said something embarrassing and sufficiently coarse to attract the "Cuckoo!" bird. But whether she said "up the butt" or "in the ass" is open to debate. I obtained a copy of the videotape and watched the clip—but Olga's response had also been bleeped out, though it's pretty obvious that she is making a salacious reference to a certain sexual act. Incidentally, even after Eubanks explained that they were talking about location, Olga was unable to come up with an answer, finally saying, "I don't know!" as a bell rang, indicating that time had run out. (Other contestants had answers such as "in the shower" and "in Canada.")

Given the evidence at hand, *The Newlywed Game* blooper would have to be considered a semi-UL. Like many other contestants during the run of the show, Olga said something that was too randy for the airwaves, in response to a question that's similar (but not identical) to the one that appears in the long-running *Newlywed Game* urban legend.

Adding to the confusion: Similar exchanges have supposedly taken place on a British TV show called *Mr. and Mrs.*, and on an Australian radio station. The dialect in these ULs is altered to fit the locales—in the British version, the woman grabs the microphone and says, "The most unusual place we've ever made love is right up the behind!" while in the Australian story, the contestant says, "Right up the arse!"—but it's essentially the same story. These seem to be wholly fictional tales, woven from a cloth that's part urban legend, part Olga.

Past Lives

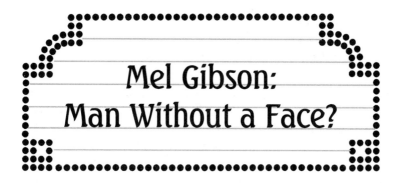

Mel Gibson:
Man Without a Face?

In July of 2000, I received an e-mail from Kate Ryan of Wilmington, Ill.:

> *Hi Rich. I got this in a forward and it's a great story. I just wonder if it's true. I've never heard it before and since you are the Urban Legend man, I thought I'd run it by you. What do ya think?*

Attached was a story I'd seen many times over the last couple of years, always attributed to the great (but sometimes gullible) Paul Harvey:

> *Years ago, a hardworking man took his family from New York State to Australia to take advantage of a work opportunity there. Part of this man's family was a handsome young son who had aspirations of joining the circus as a trapeze artist or as an*

actor. This young fellow, biding his time until a circus job or even one as a stagehand came along, worked at the local shipyards [that] bordered on the worst section of town.

Walking home from work one evening, this young man was attacked by five thugs who wanted to rob him. Instead of just giving up his money, the young fellow resisted. However, they [subdued] him easily and proceeded to beat him to a pulp. They mashed his face with their boots, and kicked and beat his body brutally with clubs, leaving him for dead. When the police happened to find him lying in the road, they assumed he was dead and called for the morgue wagon.

On the way to the morgue a policeman heard him gasp for air, and they immediately took him to the emergency unit at the hospital. When he was placed on a gurney, a nurse remarked to her horror that this young man no longer had a face. Each eye socket was smashed. His skull, legs, and arms were fractured. His nose was literally hanging from his face, all of his teeth were gone, and his jaw was almost completely torn from his skull. Although his life was spared, he spent over a year in the hospital. When he finally left, his body may have healed, but his face was disgusting to look at. He was no longer the handsome youth that everyone admired.

When the young man started to look for work again, he was turned down by everyone just because of the way he looked. One potential employer suggested to him that he join the freak show at the circus as the Man Who Had No Face. And he did this for a while. He was still rejected by everyone and no one wanted to be seen in his company. He had thoughts of suicide. This went on for five years.

One day he passed a church and sought some solace there. [Upon] entering the church, he encountered a priest who took pity on him and took him to the rectory, where they talked at great length. The priest was impressed with him to such a degree that he would do everything possible for him that could be done to restore his dignity and life, if the young man would promise to be the best Catholic he could be, and trust in God's mercy to free him from his torturous life.

The young man went to Mass and took Communion every day, and after thanking God for saving his life, asked God to only give him peace of mind and the grace to be the best man he could ever be in His eyes.

The priest, through his personal contacts, was able to secure the services of the best plastic surgeon in Australia. There would be no cost to the young man, as the doctor was the priest's best friend. The doctor, too, was impressed by the young man, whose outlook now on life was filled with good humor and love.

The surgery was a miraculous success. All the best dental work was also done for him. The young man became everything he promised God he would be. He was also blessed with a wonderful, beautiful wife, and many children, and success in the industry [that] would have been the furthest thing from his mind as a career if not for the goodness of God and the love of the people who cared for him. This he acknowledges publicly.

The young man, Mel Gibson.

His life was the inspiration for his production of the movie, The Man Without a Face. *He is to be admired by all of us as a God-fearing man, a political conservative, and an example to all as a true man of courage.*

First let's poke our fingers through some of the holes in this story. If Mel Gibson has been publicly acknowledging this story, how did we all miss it? Wasn't anyone watching Leno or Letterman when Mel told this unbelievably heart-wrenching tale?

And what's the deal with that priest? Apparently, he was not only best friends with a miracle-working plastic surgeon, but he had the best dental connections as well? Where was this guy a pastor, at Our Lady of Perpetual Cosmetic Makeovers?

Also, the 1993 movie *The Man Without a Face* doesn't follow the Paul Harvey plot at all. Directed by and starring Gibson, the adaptation of a novel by Isabelle Holland is the story of a man who is badly burned in an automobile accident and is something of a scary legend in his hometown—the subject of many urban legends, as a matter of fact. (Some say he killed his wife; others say he murdered a child.) When the disfigured man strikes up a friendship with a local boy, the narrow-minded townsfolk are suspicious of the nature of this relationship and the police chief steps in.

The folksy Paul Harvey apparently doesn't have a cynical hair on his head, and he has broadcast a number of urban legends as true anecdotes—everything from Al Gore's supposed misreading of a biblical quote in a speech to the story of a woman who sunbathed in the nude atop a skylight to the bogus version of Jane Fonda's Hanoi visit to the "celebrity snub." But this time, Harvey is getting a bad rap. He has never uttered a word about *The Man Without a Face* legend, even though his name is almost always attached to the story and he's even "credited" with providing the story to an "anti-bullying" Web site.

For the record: The story is completely false. The only morsel of similar experience to be found in Gibson's past is the tale that he was in a barroom brawl just before his audition for the *Mad Max* movies and sustained a few cuts and bruises—which, if anything, probably helped him get the part of the road warrior. (Incidentally, Gibson is a practicing Catholic who regularly attends Mass, but to his credit, he rarely discusses his faith in interviews. His private life remains private.)

In the December 14, 2000 edition of *USA Today*, Gibson answered questions from readers as part of his promotional tour for *What Women Want*. Judy McClintock of Lead, S.D., wrote: "I read (via e-mail, so how reliable is that?) that Paul

Harvey reported you were badly beaten and left for dead as a young man in Australia, so badly scarred that you worked in a circus act, inspiring the movie *The Man Without a Face*. The article stated that a Catholic priest was very instrumental in helping to put your face, body, and life back together. How much truth was in that?"

Gibson's reply: "It was a total concoction, one of those Internet things. It's a complete fabrication. Paul Harvey never aired it. I was overhauled with plastic surgery? It's just a lot of bunk...."

Bunk written by somebody with an agenda. (Poorly written, I might add. The story I reprinted is a cleaned-up version with many errors in spelling, grammar, and simple logic improved. The first time I saw the story, it was virtually unreadable.) Note that Gibson's good fortune is ascribed to his faith and to the good graces of that priest; his family conveniently disappears from the saga the moment he is injured. And the closing passage that mentions that Gibson is a "political conservative" comes out of left—or should I say, right—field. What does that have to do with anything?

Whoever penned this apocryphal tale wanted to make a strong endorsement for the Christian faith and right-wing politics.

Bogart the Gerber Baby?

By most accounts, ultimate movie tough guy Humphrey Bogart was born on Christmas Day, 1899—although some authorities, including the Lauren Bacall book *The Complete Films of Humphrey Bogart*, claim Bogie was born earlier that year and that Warner Bros. changed the date for publicity purposes.

Bogie certainly wouldn't have been the first, or the last, movie star to have his birthday (or birth year) moved in accordance with a studio's wishes, but Bacall's book does talk about celebrating Bogart's birthday on Christmas. And according to the book *Bogart* by A.M. Sperber and Eric Lax, the *Ontario* (Ohio) *County Times* of January 10, 1900, carried a birth announcement listing Humphrey's first big entrance as December 25, 1899. And I doubt that even Warner Bros. of the 1930s would have had a reach that extended all the way to the clippings library of the *Ontario County Times*.

What's beyond dispute is that Bogie's dad, DeForest, was a Manhattan surgeon, and his mom, Maud Humphrey Bogart, was a successful commercial illustrator who did work for *Harpers* and other popular magazines of the time. From the 1890s through the 1920s, Mrs. Bogart often drew portraits of socialite children, using a Victorian-influenced style that emphasized cherubic features. It stands to reason that a mother with such a specific talent would want to use her own son as a model, and in fact, Bogart was the model for Mellin's Baby Food, among other products.

Given all that, it's easy to see how so many people could come to believe that Bogart was also the original Gerber baby, the model for an image that, even today, is one of the most famous and well-liked baby portraits in all the world.

But it's not true.

When I tried to refute the Bogie–Gerber story in my *Chicago Sun-Times* column a few years ago, I was surprised at the volume of responses I received from agitated readers who were adamant in their belief that I was just plain wrong. Many of them urged me to print a correction and take my medicine like a man, because the evidence was irrefutable that Bogart, indeed, was the original Gerber baby.

I'm still breathlessly awaiting that evidence. In the meantime, I'll stick with time-line reality.

As we've already established, Bogart was born at the turn of the century. The Gerber company, however, was not born at the turn of the century. The company was launched in the Gerber family kitchen in 1927, when Daniel and Dorothy Gerber were trying to strain peas for their daughter and came up with the idea of doing it at the family-owned canning plant. By the following year, Daniel Gerber had produced mass quantities of several baby food flavors, and the company began national distribution.

That means that Humphrey Bogart was on the verge of turning 30 by the time anyone really heard of Gerber baby food.

The company wouldn't use his face for a baby food then unless they were trying to scare people away!

Of course, it's conceivable that somebody at Gerber could have come across one of Maud Bogart's old drawings of Humphrey and used it on the original jars. But there's no evidence that such an event occurred—whereas there's a mountain of evidence, and even a court ruling, that supports the claims that the Gerber baby is one Ann Turner Cook.

Dorothy Hope Smith, a family friend of the Cooks, submitted a charcoal drawing of the 4-month-old Cook to Gerber in 1928, and the company made that drawing the centerpiece of its ad campaign. That image hasn't changed much over the years, despite rumors that the likes of Jane Seymour and Brooke Shields have been infant models for an "updated" version of the Gerber baby.

In the 1940s, Gerber was taken to court by a parent who claimed his child was the real Gerber baby. But the judge ruled that the baby in the original sketch by Smith was the Gerber baby and ruled in favor of the company.

As for Gerber baby Ann Turner Cook, now 74, she's a retired schoolteacher living in Florida. According to a 1997 article in the *St. Petersburg Times*, Cook and her husband were able to pay for their college tuition and buy a new car in the late 1940s with the residuals she earned from being the original Gerber baby.

In a telephone interview for this book, Cook said, "My mother, now 96, was a close friend of the artist who made the drawing. My father was an artist. When I was a baby, Dorothy made a good many drawings of me. Her technique was to take movie film, and then stop the film on an expression that she wanted [and draw from that]. That film has long [since] disappeared. [But] she thought I was a good subject. And [Gerber] used the sketch just as it was drawn, with no refinements.

"The Bogart rumor...somehow got into a trivia game. I've heard other celebrities mentioned, even Elizabeth Taylor!

People don't expect the Gerber baby to be someone who turned out to be a high school English teacher. I'm 74 now, so let's say that time has taken a little bit of a toll. I'm told by people that the resemblance is marked when they see me. [I think] most of us look a little bit like our baby pictures."

Cook said she doesn't mind that some people think Bogie was the Gerber baby, but it has always bothered her that Dorothy Hope Smith didn't get more attention.

"It's an urban legend—these things get legs of their own. [But] I wish the artist had gotten more credit for it. I met her only a couple of times as an adult; she died in 1955. I always felt she should get the credit, because all babies are adorable [but she] captured the appeal a baby has."

As for Maud Humphrey Bogart's bouncing baby boy, he did all right for himself—but his credits do *not* include jars of baby food. Here's looking at someone other than you, kid.

Humphrey Bogart is one of the foremost legends in cinematic history, so it's only fitting that he should be the star (or a supporting player) in more than one urban legend. Following are a couple of other Bogie-related ULs. (A full discussion of the Ronald Reagan/*Casblanca* urban legend can be found in the "Movies" section of this book.)

BOGIE HAD A YOUNGER BROTHER NAMED ED—ED SULLIVAN, THAT IS.

The sour-faced Sullivan did have a slight facial resemblance to Bogie—but they were not related. Bogart had two sisters, but no brothers.

**BOGART'S MOST FAMOUS AND MOST IMITATED MOVIE
LINE IS, "PLAY IT AGAIN, SAM."**

Maybe so, but he never utters that exact line in *Casablanca* or in any other movie.

★ ★ ★

**BOGART'S LISP WAS FROM AN INJURY HE SUSTAINED
WHILE IN THE NAVY.**

Well, maybe. Bogart enlisted in the U.S. Navy in 1918. One story says that Bogart was taking a prisoner to a Portsmouth Naval Prison in New Hampshire when the handcuffed prisoner cracked Bogie in the mouth and started running. (Bogie supposedly chased down the prisoner and knocked him cold with the butt of his gun.) In another version, his lip was ripped by a piece of shrapnel when his ship, the U.S.S. *Leviathan*, was under fire in World War I. But some biographies of Bogart assert that the injury occurred much earlier in Bogart's life—when he was 10 years old—and his father hit him.

**WARNER BROS. THREATENED TO SUE THE MARX BROTHERS
FOR COPYRIGHT INFRINGEMENT WHEN THE STUDIO LEARNED
ABOUT THEIR PLANS TO MAKE *A NIGHT IN CASABLANCA*.**

It's true that Warner Bros. expressed some concern when rumors surfaced that the Marx Brothers' movie would have characters with names like "Humphrey Bogus," but the supposed lawsuit was really a publicity stunt concocted by the Marx Brothers that enabled Groucho to fire off a number of hilarious letters to the studio, with comments such as, "You probably have the right to use the name Warner, but what about Brothers? Professionally, we were brothers long before you were!" Somehow these letters were leaked to the papers, giving the Marx Brothers and their new film tons of free publicity.

Did the Duke
Dodge the Draft?

John Wayne was soused. Not slightly cheery, not charmingly inebriated, but hammered.

This was circa 1970. The Duke was addressing a group of ROTC students and he was royally pissed off about the anti-Vietnam War protests that were taking place on campuses nationwide. Slurring his words like a bad actor playing a drunk in a road show of *Paint Your Wagon*, Wayne expressed disgust with the way of the world.

"I went to school at the University of Southern California," he said during his speech. "When I went there, there was a fella in control of the college. He was the boss man there. If anybody had walked into, his, uh, office, and torn down the picture...or written lewd words on the pictures of his family, we as members of the college would have kicked the hell out of his organization. I don't give a shit if you go to the school or not, you can't stand to have this happen."

There was a smattering of applause, but Wayne said, "Oh Christ, I'm not trying to talk for clapping, I'm trying to talk for you guys. You better start thinking. It's getting to be re-goddamn-diculous. If you guys don't start thinking as men, we're going to have a lousy country. Jesus! They're trying to wreck our goddamn country. It's time for you younger guys to take over, I don't know what the hell to do."

That speech might sound like an urban legend, but I know it to be true because I've heard a recording of it. (The Wayne tirade and many other classic sound bites of famous people caught with their guard down is available on a two-volume CD called *Celebrities at Their Worst*. Look for it on the Internet.) Of course, the Duke never was shy about voicing his support for American involvement in the Vietnam War—and his disdain for anyone who had the temerity to speak out against the war. Wayne saw things in the same black-and-white hues as his early films, and in his eyes, anyone who was against the war was also against Mom, baseball, apple pie, and the American way. It was this blind patriotism that steered Wayne to direct and star in *The Green Berets* (1968), a piece of jingoistic nonsense so one-sided and dogmatic it makes Leni Riefenstahl's *Triumph of the Will* look like a balanced view of the Nazi movement. In the movie, Wayne plays a Special Forces Colonel who leads his troops into battle and convinces the liberal journalist (played by David Janssen) that this is a just war, after all.

The Green Berets is one of the execrable pieces of propaganda in cinema history—but John Wayne looked good in that Special Forces uniform and that jaunty green beret, as tough and solid and brave as he had come across more than two decades earlier in films such as *The Sands of Iwo Jima, Flying Tigers,* and *War of the Wildcats.* From sea to shining sea, or at least from studio lot to shining studio lot, Wayne proudly wore the stars and stripes during World War II as he fought with honor for his country in countless films that always, always showed the Americans coming out on top.

Some would say his celluloid patriotism through the years earned him the right to mock and belittle the hippies and yippies and bums who burned their draft cards, protested the war, or fled to Canada or college to avoid military service. Others would say that Wayne was a four-star hypocrite, because the so-called American hero who once received a Congressional Gold Medal was never in any branch of the military and actually went to great lengths to stay out of the service during World War II, while other great stars of the era dutifully enlisted and served with honor.

That's right. John Wayne was a draft dodger.

Or was he? Wayne was not a veteran; that we know for sure. And there's overwhelming evidence to prove he did go to some lengths to stay out of the service during the war years—but a gathering of all the facts indicates that the "draft dodger" label is a harsh and unfair exaggeration, if not a borderline urban legend.

Let's take a look at the career that Wayne had carved out in the years before the war. For most of the 1930s he was doing grunt work in hack Westerns and adventure stories—long-forgotten movies like *Ride Him, Cowboy*; *Randy Rides Alone;* and the immortal *Western Double Feature 2.* (Wayne wasn't in the first *Western Double Feature*, but he did pop up in *Western Double Feature 3*, probably my favorite of the trilogy.) By the end of the decade, Wayne was past 30 years of age and his shot at stardom had seemingly passed him by—until he grabbed a starring role in 1939's *Stagecoach,* the classic Western from John Ford, that vaulted Wayne onto the A-list.

When the Japanese bombed Pearl Harbor in 1941, Wayne was in his mid-30s and had just begun to enjoy the trappings of success. His USC football days had left him a little banged up, but he was still a strapping and relatively young specimen who wouldn't have been turned down by the draft board on the basis of his physical condition. However, Wayne was also married, and he had four children. So, like thousands of other men in similar situations, he applied for and was given 3-A status, meaning he was allowed a deferment for reasons of family dependency. (Even after a couple of decent paychecks for his initial headliner roles, Wayne was far from wealthy at the time.)

Interesting, though, that a number of Wayne's peers—including some with families and some who were about his age—did sign up. Clark Gable, who was born in 1901; Henry Fonda, who was born in 1905; and Jimmy Stewart, who was born in 1908, all served their country, while Wayne (born in 1907) did all of his fighting with the cameras rolling. The closest he came to any real soldiers was when he entertained troops in the Pacific on a USO tour in 1943 and 1944.

But let the record show that Wayne was cheered mightily by the troops on that tour, and his patriotic films were greatly appreciated as morale boosters for the boys. It could be argued that a John Wayne in his mid-to-late 30s with a wife and four children was of much better use as a Hollywood cheerleader and financial provider to his family than he would have been as, say, a member of John Ford's photography unit in the U.S. Navy.

Wayne certainly must have thought so. Not only did he shuffle his feet at Ford's invitation to join the Navy, but he applied for and received a 2-A classification (he wanted a deferment in the "national interest") in 1944, and he turned to his studio for help when he was later reclassified as 1-A. The studio responded, and soon he was safe again under the 2-A umbrella.

What it comes down to is this: There was no physical injury that prevented Wayne from joining up and he aggressively avoided active duty—but he was certainly within his rights to obtain the deferments he got.

This does not mean that Wayne was a coward. It means that he was an ordinary man who did what he could to stay out of a foxhole. Whether or not that makes him a hypocrite is something for the real veterans of real wars to decide.

Here's a look at a few other urban legends in which the Duke has starred or played a supporting role:

WAYNE WAS THE FIRST CHOICE TO PLAY MARSHAL DILLON IN *GUNSMOKE*.

In the 1950s and 1960s, the actors and behind-the-scenes people who worked in the motion picture industry looked down, way down, on the television industry. With few exceptions, anyone who made the move from films to TV was doing so out of necessity, not choice. (These days, though film is still considered the supreme medium, many stars have hopped back and forth from movies to TV series with no major drop-off in perceived career status.) Sure, a film vet such as Lucille Ball would leap at the chance at her own TV show, but a Marilyn Monroe, an Audrey Hepburn? No way.

Same thing with John Wayne. Although his career had its dips after he hit it big in 1939, he was always thought of as a larger-than-life, and larger-than-the-small-screen, kind of star—and he definitely thought of himself that way. And let's not forget that Wayne didn't win his Oscar until 1970 for *True*

Grit, and that he was still making films as late as three years before his death, his last effort being the 1976 dying-gunfighter flick, *The Shootist*. At any point in his career, Wayne would have been too pricey, too proud, and *too damn big* to even be offered a role on a Western TV series—a role he would have turned down instantly if anyone had been crazy enough to make the offer in the first place. The Marshal Dillon part, of course, went to James Arness, whose major contribution to American cinema to that point had been the title role in *The Thing*.

WAYNE WAS SUCH A MEAT-EATING FIEND THAT, WHEN HE DIED, HIS AUTOPSY REVEALED **40** POUNDS OF IMPACTED FECAL MATTER LODGED IN HIS COLON.

Vegetarians love to spout this story as evidence of the evils of ingesting dead cows and other meats. Elvis Presley's name has also been invoked in this nauseating bit of folklore—but with Elvis, the number grows to 60 or even an astounding 80 pounds. Gross! And completely beyond the realm of medical possibility. Imagine—just for a moment, so the picture doesn't stay lodged in your brain—what someone would look like if 40 or 60 or 80 pounds of anything were lodged in his midsection. He'd look to be about 65 months pregnant, for crying out loud.

Speaking of which, he would literally be crying out loud, to say the least. Even a buildup of a pound or two of the aforementioned substance would severely damage the bowel muscles and would cause great pain to the afflicted individual. The Duke (or the King) would have been in a hospital long before the poundage reached such an astronomical number. Presley's autopsy did indicate a jam-packed digestive system, but it was due to his abuse of drugs, not his love of cheeseburgers.

Wayne underwent surgery for an intestinal blockage a few months before his death in 1979; perhaps that is the foundation for this UL. In any event, no autopsy was necessary when he passed away, as he was a septuagenarian cancer patient who had died of natural causes.

Cher's
Rib Removal

By Cher's own admission, she's undergone cosmetic surgery on her nose and breasts, and she's had her teeth fixed. But some cynical and snickering observers insist that she's had a lot more work done than that. The stories and rumors about Cher going under the knife are so rife that she's become the poster celebrity for plastic surgery jokes, as when Jay Leno did a skit on *The Tonight Show* about "lesser known laws in America" and said, "Construction work will not begin on Cher before 8 a.m., so as not to disturb her neighbors."

Ouch!

Who knows whether Cher has had cheek implants, collagen injections, liposuction, an eye job, or a buttocks lift for that matter? As long as she never again wears the Indian getup she donned to sing "Half-Breed" in the 1970s, she's all right by me.

The most persistent claim about Cher's bodywork is that she underwent a bizarre procedure to slim her figure—she had two ribs removed.

From Dr. Miriam Stoppard's advice column in the November 3, 2000, edition of the *London Daily Mirror*:

> *There are many well-publicised examples of very beautiful women feeling inadequate, despite universal acclaim for their beauty. Brigitte Bardot, can you imagine it, thought she was fat! Marilyn Monroe had a lifelong anxiety about Elizabeth Taylor being more beautiful, as if anyone could compare with her on her own terms. Cher, even when she was young, slender, and incredibly beautiful, had ribs removed because she thought her waist needed narrowing. It's sad, but often true, that being in love makes some women feel insecure and vulnerable no matter what their attributes.*

A praiseworthy message, but it's partially based on lousy information. Despite the unfounded stories about women in Victorian times undergoing rib removal surgery to achieve 18" waistlines, there's no indication that Cher, or any other human being since Adam, has voluntarily had ribs removed to facilitate a slim look. (Urban lore has it that weirdo shock rocker Marilyn Manson, who kinda looks like Cher if you've had a couple of Cosmopolitans and if the lighting is just wrong, also had a rib removed. Not so he'd look slimmer, but so he'd be limber enough to be able to orally please himself. My apologies for sharing that mental image with you.) It's amazing that such a ridiculous story could be accepted by so many people who should know better. How in the world would a rib-removal operation be an improvement, anyway? Would the surgeon crack a couple of ribs from the rib cage? And wouldn't such a grotesque and severe procedure leave serious scars that would sort of defeat the purpose? *Ooh, that Cher is so skinny. And don't those scars go nicely with her tattoos?*

In 1988, the magazine *Paris Match* printed the urban legend as fact, and had to run a correction after Cher filed a lawsuit against the magazine. But as we've learned with other urban legends—and sometimes even with entire books about urban legends—the stories debunking the false tales are sometimes mistakenly cited by people as confirmation of the UL. People read something about "Cher" and "ribs removed" and they somehow forget that words and phrases like "untrue" and "unfounded" and "we regret the error" were also in the story.

Cher herself has confronted this rumor head-on for years, in a number of interviews:

"I've read for years that I've had a rib removed in order to look better in tight-fitting costumes," she told Cindy Pearlman, an entertainment writer for my newspaper, the *Chicago Sun-Times*, in April of 2000. "Medically, I don't think this is even a possibility," she added.

"I'm a tabloid person's dream," Cher told *US* magazine in February of 2000. "If someone said, 'Whitney Houston had her ribs removed,' you'd go, 'That's ridiculous!' If someone said, 'Cher had her ribs removed,' everybody would go, 'You know, I heard that, too.'"

She's got a point. Cher's consistently flamboyant antics and her willingness to admit to at least some cosmetic surgery makes her a likely target for gossip and wild stories. ("I have done some controversial things in my life, so I'm an easy target," she acknowledged to the *Providence Journal-Bulletin* in a 1999 interview. "People are more willing to believe that I would do crazy things, because in my life I really have done crazy things.") Logic should tell anyone that the rib removal story has to be bunk—but if anyone would undergo such a procedure, it would be Cher, not Marie Osmond.

"I've had my cheekbones since I was small," Cher told the *London Daily Telegraph* in January of 1999, as she addressed rumors of countless surgeries. "And it is impossible to have a rib removed! That always seemed particularly silly to me—but I will have to defend myself for the rest of my life against it."

If it's any consolation to Cher, the ribs-removed UL seems to be making its way to the next generation. Younger actresses and models such as Lara Flynn Boyle, Calista Flockhart, Stephanie Seymour, and Tori Spelling have had their names attached to the rib tale.

"Once I read that I had my ribs removed to make me skinny," Spelling told *Harper's Bazaar* in 1999. "Then again, I read an article a couple of years ago that Cher had her ribs removed, and I believed it. So why wouldn't people believe it?"

Hanoi
Jane Fonda

I n the winter of 1999, the campaign against Jane Fonda's selection as one of the "100 Greatest Women of the Century" was in high gear. Thousands of anti-Fonda activists, many of them Vietnam veterans, were flooding the media with petitions and letters protesting the choice of "Hanoi Jane" as an American icon who would be toasted in a Barbara Walters special on ABC-TV. There was even talk about a boycott against the network and its parent company, Disney.

The long-standing resentment against Fonda is understandable. For many veterans of the Vietnam War, Fonda will always be the spoiled, Hollywood rich-kid brat who snuggled up to the enemy during her tour of North Vietnam in 1972, posing for pictures while peering into the sights of an NVA antiaircraft artillery launcher; touring villages and hospitals and schools, broadcasting her anti-American-involvement views over Radio Hanoi and telling the world that American POWs were being treated with care and respect. A few years later, Fonda said POWs returning home with stories of physical torture and systematic psychological abuse were "hypocrites and liars."

Ms. Fonda, I'd like to see you tell that to Sen. John McCain, a man who, to this day, cannot comb his own hair because of the torture he endured while held in a bamboo cage for more than five years.

However well-intentioned it might have been, Fonda's incredibly naive and offensive stance against the Vietnam War was utterly polluted by her unforgivable and morally hollow attacks against the good, mostly working class and poor American men and women who were sent off to fight that war. No matter what she has done since then, for many vets and patriots, she'll always be "Hanoi Jane" (which explains why in the year 2001, a men's room urinal at one of the places where I work is decorated with a strategically placed sticker of Ms. Fonda in an aerobics outfit).

As the year 1999 was drawing to a close, we were awash in lists of the greatest this or the worst that of the 20th century, in every category imaginable. Given Fonda's radical activist legacy, it was no surprise that so many Americans were agitated over the news that she would be honored on the Walters special as one of the pioneering American females of the 1900s, right up there with real heroes such as Eleanor Roosevelt and Rachel Carson. Here's an excerpt from one of the e-mails that was in heavy rotation on the Internet:

ABC is allowing Barbara Walters to honor Jane Fonda in a special on "100 Women of the Century." Shame, shame, shame on Barbara Walters! And shame, shame, shame on the Disney Company.

Let us not forget what Jane Fonda did to this country at a vulnerable time in our nation's history.

In 1972, several American POWs were dragged out of captivity, cleaned up, given fresh clothes, and paraded in front of Miss Fonda. One POW, Air Force pilot Jerry Driscoll, spat on her—and for this 'injustice' he was beaten so badly he nearly died, and to this day suffers from double vision.

Still, many of the POWs hoped against hope that Fonda had a shred of compassion for them. Wishing to get some kind of word back to their families, each man had secreted a tiny piece of paper, with his Social Security number on it, in the palm of his hand. As Fonda walked the line of prisoners, she said things like, "Aren't you sorry you bombed babies?" and "Are you grateful for the humane treatment you're getting from your benevolent captors?" Believing this had to be an act, the prisoners each palmed her their scraps of paper. She took them all without missing a beat, never acknowledging what was happening—thus giving the prisoners hope that she would indeed deliver the information to their loved ones. But at the end of the line, after the cameras had stopped rolling, Fonda turned to the officer in charge—AND HANDED HIM THE PILE OF PAPERS!!!!

Three men died from the subsequent beatings they received. Shame! Shame! Shame! Please forward this message to as many people as possible, and contact ABC and Disney to let them know you don't think Jane Fonda should be on anybody's list of the "100 Greatest Women."

In a nationally syndicated column published in November of 1999, William F. Buckley ranted: "Somebody, somewhere, is making up a list of the 100 Women of the Century, and the name of Jane Fonda has been submitted for consideration." Buckley recounted the stories about Fonda and the line of prisoners, said the report in the e-mail "was nothing if not concrete" (although in the next breath he acknowledged that "the Internet communication does not give [sources]"), and expressed his outrage that "Jane Fonda is not up for a treason trial, she is up for a 100 Greatest Women award."

But everyone was getting upset about something that: 1) wasn't going to happen, and, 2) never did happen.

Fonda did visit Hanoi in 1972 and did participate in an obscene spectacle of misplaced defiance—but the oft-repeated story about her comments to the POWs, her betrayal of them, and the deaths of the three soldiers contains not a shred of truth.

Larry Carrigan, one of the officers whose name often appears in the "Hanoi Jane" e-mails ("three officers died, but a fourth, Col. Larry Carrigan, survived to tell this story"), has gone on record as saying he has no knowledge of the supposed incident.

"It's a figment of somebody's imagination," Lt. Carrigan told David Emery, who runs the *Urban Legends and Folklore* Web site at about.com. "I never met Jane Fonda."

Jerry Driscoll, the POW who is said to have spat at Fonda during her visit, also says it never happened. "It's the product of a very vivid imagination," he told Emery.

Mike McGrath, former president of NAM-POWs, told Emery he thinks Fonda is a "traitorous witch" and said, "We all hate her as much as the next person," but added, "You need to get your stories straight. There were never any POWs killed on account of Jane."

When McGrath was contacted for this book, he reaffirmed that the story is pure urban legend: "Driscoll...was my roomie in Hanoi, [and] I've talked with Carrigan. Both confirm that the statements attributed to them did not occur. Someone made up the story about the strips of paper, POWs being betrayed, killed, etc. This is an Internet hoax story."

In 1988, Fonda delivered a televised apology for her actions. Since then, she has said many times that her actions were "thoughtless and careless." Nevertheless, many regarded her apologies as too little, too cynical, and way, way too late.

As for the Barbara Walters special, by the time the e-mails about Fonda were making the rounds, it had already aired—on April 30, 1999. It was called *A Celebration: 100 Years of Great Women*, and it was based on a *Ladies Home Journal* coffee-table book titled *The 100 Most Important Women of the Century*. And yes, Fonda was included in that roster. The distinction may be lost on some, but there is a difference between "great" and "important." Fonda may not fit your definition of "great"—she certainly doesn't fit mine—but it could be argued that her work as an actress and as a controversial lightning rod of the 1960s would qualify her as someone of importance, just as other notorious and morally bankrupt figures are often cited as "influential."

The "Hanoi Jane" urban legend is a pop culture cocktail consisting of fact, partially correct information, and pure mythology. But if anyone had compiled a list of the 100 Most Disgraceful Acts by Celebrities in the 20th Century, Fonda's documented behavior while she was in Hanoi would have been more than enough to place her high on the list.

As McGrath puts is, "Fonda did enough bad things to assure her a correct place in the garbage dumps of history. We don't want to be party to false stories [that] could be used as an excuse that her real actions didn't happen either."

Marilyn's Dress Size

"I've always thought Marilyn Monroe looked fabulous, but I'd kill myself if I was that fat." —ACTRESS ELIZABETH HURLEY

"Look at Marilyn Monroe, though, size 16 and gorgeous." —ACTRESS KATE WINSLET

"Marilyn Monroe was huge. When she put her hand on her hip, it disappeared." —COSTUME DESIGNER LISA JENSEN

"I'm more sexy than Pamela Lee or whoever else they've got out these days. Marilyn Monroe was a size 16. That says it all." —ROSEANNE

Indeed it does say it all, Roseanne. It says that our culture is so obsessed with unrealistic female body images that nearly 40 years after Marilyn Monroe's death, her dress size remains the subject of hot debate and is used to bolster all manner of weight-related arguments, from "Marilyn was too fat" to "Marilyn at that weight would never be a star in today's world" to "If a size 16 is good enough for Marilyn, it should be good enough for me."

It's too easy to assert that Hollywood sex symbols in the 1940s and 1950s were healthier and more realistically voluptuous than today's anorexic, implanted goddesses. Sure, women such as Marilyn and Sophia Loren and Rita Hayworth were soft and gorgeous and curvaceous; they wouldn't have been interested in sculpting "abs of steel" even if they knew what abs of steel were. But let's not forget that the stick-thin Audrey Hepburn was considered to be just as much a feminine ideal back then as any of the aforementioned sex symbols. And while the waif look, aka "heroin chic," made superstars in the 1990s out of models such as Kate Moss, and big TV stars out of Popsicle-shaped actresses such as Calista Flockhart and Lara Flynn Boyle and Courteney Cox, today's news organizations have scrutinized these women's figures relentlessly and critically over the last several years. Commentators have not been shy about reflecting what much of the general public feels about these gals, i.e., they look unwell. Meanwhile, beautiful but softer-bodied women such as Kate Winslet and Alicia Silverstone, and heavier gals such as Camryn Mannheim and Delta Burke, are cheered for publicly embracing their very normal physical profiles.

Of course, for every actress who appears to have accepted that she'll never be a size 0, there are probably a hundred who truly believe they'd be getting better parts if they only lost five more pounds—and there's no shortage of producers, directors, agents, and managers who will reinforce that belief every chance they get.

So women turn to Marilyn's legacy for a bit of comfort. A size 16 and yet she was the greatest sex symbol of her era!

If only it were true.

You'd think that finding out Marilyn Monroe's actual dress size would be an easy task. However, because she had clothes custom made, because her measurements fluctuated as she matured and as she battled addiction, and because women's dress sizes today don't correlate to women's dress sizes in the 1950s, it is impossible to definitively state Marilyn's dress size with the degree of certainty that one could state, say, her height—except to say that she was probably never a "true" size 16.

This much we know about Monroe. She was 5'5½" tall, and she usually weighed between 120 and 135 pounds. Her bust was in the 36"- to 37"-range, her waist was usually listed at 22" or 23", her hips at 35" to 37".

And she wore a size 36-D bra.

We also have an exhaustive visual record of Marilyn's figure, from the time she was an unknown redhead posing for a calendar shot that became a *Playboy* centerfold through her years of superstardom and her final sad months. In the calendar shot, Monroe is downright lithe; in some later films and newsreel footage, she's slightly jiggly. Most of the time she looked curvy and sexy. She had hips. She had breasts. Maybe a rounded tummy. But I've yet to come across a photograph or a single frame of film in which MM is truly zaftig.

Refer back to those measurements for a moment. As any woman can tell you, a size 22 or 23 waist does *not* require a size 16 dress. (The tight-as-a-second-skin dress Monroe wore in *Some Like It Hot* is on display in a museum in London and has a 26" waist—but some biographers claim that Monroe was pregnant during the making of that movie. And even a 26" waist i s quite svelte.) Some accounts from the 1950s list Monroe as 37-24-37. If she had been standing next to Audrey Hepburn she would have looked like an hourglass filled with puppies, but those numbers are still far from Shelley Winters territory. (And let it be noted that Ms. Winters had it goin' on when she was younger.) Other reports from the time list Monroe's measurements as 35-22-35.

I once toured the now-shuttered Debbie Reynolds Hotel and Museum in Las Vegas, which included a collection of about a dozen of Marilyn's dresses, including the famous "subway grate" white dress from *The Seven Year Itch*. They ranged from a size 4 to a size 8, in today's sizes.

Most likely, the largest dress Monroe ever wore was a size 12—and a size 12 in the 1950s would be more like a size 8 by today's standards. Even if she did wear a size 16 back then, that would make her a size 12 in 2001.

Do not ask me why the standards for dress sizes have changed so much. I'm sure it has to do with designers trying to make women feel less fat, which will lead to more sales. For that matter, do not ask me why a size 8 dress by one designer is the exact match of a size 12 by someone else. All I know is, far too many women spend more time obsessing about dress size than they do almost any other number in their lives, from IQ to checking account balance. If it helps to believe that the most enduring Hollywood sex symbol of the 20th century wore a size 16 dress, let the urban legend live on.

MOVIES

Fargo-ing
the Truth

*P*remiere magazine: "How close was the script [for *Fargo*] to the actual event?"

Ethan Coen: "Pretty close."

Rent the classic comedy-mystery-thriller *Fargo* or catch it on cable some night, and you'll see this opening title card:

> *This is a true story. The events depicted in this film took place in Minnesota in 1987. At the request of the survivors, the names have been changed. Out of respect for the dead, the rest has been told exactly as it occurred.*

When I saw *Fargo* for the first time, I was quickly enveloped in its quirky, dark charm, which resonated all the more with me because I believed I was actually watching a fictionalized rendition of events that really occurred. As the story unraveled, I couldn't wait to find the newspaper articles or perhaps even a book that would fill me in on the "real" story of Chief Gunderson (whatever her true name might be) and her pursuit of the corrupt auto dealer Jerry Lundegaard and the two psychotic lumps of evil he had hired to kidnap his wife.

Turns out the joke was on me. There were no articles to be found in the archives of the Minnesota papers, nor had any books been written about the supposed kidnapping scam in 1987 that went haywire and eventually led to seven murders in various Minnesota towns.

That's because none of that stuff ever happened. *Fargo* was 100-percent fiction, and the "true story" ruse was just another practical joke from those wacky Coen brothers, Joel and Ethan.

The Coens have a reputation for playing around with the facts—and with the media—in this fashion. For example, even though they edit their own movies, they've created a fictional editor named Roderick Jaynes—a pompous sort who has supposedly written the introduction for the printed versions of some Coen scripts and has talked up his contributions to *Barton Fink* and *Miller's Crossing* while subtly jabbing Ethan and Joel.

Still, one can't really fault the scores of reviewers and feature writers who believed *Fargo* was based in reality. Strange and Byzantine as the story was, it wasn't any more bizarre than some of the true-life crime stories we hear about all the time. And even the production notes in the press kit said it was a true story.

And so *Premiere* magazine called *Fargo* a "true-life tale," and *Film Threat* magazine said *Fargo* was "based on a true tale of a botched kidnapping," and the movie critic for the *Orlando Sentinel* wrote:

"'This is a true story,' explains an introductory note. And as eccentric as the new film is, its story indeed rings true. In most movies about real events, the filmmakers leave out information that would get in the way of the main story line. But one of *Fargo*'s strengths is that the odd, awkward details don't appear to have been airbrushed away...."

Even the *South China Post* got into the act, in a 1996 review: "*Fargo*, then, is a different kind of project, based on an actual event that took place in Minnesota, in the American Midwest, in 1987."

But some enterprising reporters started doing some checking, and it was quickly apparent that *Fargo* wasn't any more reality-based than *The Wizard of Oz*.

First, there's not a single person in Minnesota who can remember anything like the plot of *Fargo* unfolding in real life in the 1980s. (You'd think people in a small town like Brainerd, Minn., would remember things like a cop getting shot and an auto salesman arranging for his wife's kidnapping and a string of murders—not to mention the pregnant police chief who eventually brought the killers to justice.) As statistician Kathleen Leatherman of the Minnesota Bureau of Criminal Apprehension told the *Minneapolis Star-Tribune,* "This is major fiction. There were no officers killed in 1987...There's nothing that even vaguely relates to these circumstances."

I'd still put *Fargo* on my list of the 100 greatest American movies; it's an original and sly piece of work charged with terrific writing, faultless pacing, and a smart cast, led by Frances McDormand in her Oscar-winning performance. But I wonder: Would it have been quite so captivating that first time I saw it had I not been under the mistaken impression that it was based on a true story? I'll never know. The experience is locked in the past and cannot be revised.

In a way, the Coen brothers' dishonest little joke backfired on them. The minor tempest created by the "Is it real or not?" investigations, and the subsequent articles about the controversy, served as a minor distraction from what should have been a pure celebration of innovative filmmaking. The legacy of *Fargo* was ever-so-slightly bruised by the brothers' lie, and they have only themselves to blame.

Sometimes you can be just a little too clever for your own good.

Briefcase Full of Soul

Q uentin Tarantino's groundbreaking and exhilarating masterpiece *Pulp Fiction* is the kind of movie you can watch again and again, discovering new pleasures each time. The overlapping and time-shifting storylines, the attention to the smallest background details, the oft-quoted dialogue, the surf music soundtrack, and the wonderful performances from the all-star cast make this one of the best and most influential films of the 1990s.

At the heart of the movie is a briefcase that men will kill for. When one has this briefcase in his possession and opens it for the first time to behold the glowing miracle inside, he is reduced to speechless awe.

So what's inside the briefcase? The characters never get specific about it. They say things like, "Is that what I think it is?"—and the movie never shows us. (Every shot of the brief-case is from behind its open lid. We see people react to it as the contents give off a golden glow.) But that hasn't stopped some aficionados of Tarantino's work from asserting that they know *exactly* what's inside.

A frequently posted Internet message:

If you all are anything like me, then you had no idea what was in the briefcase in Pulp Fiction. *But there's no longer any mystery about what's inside the briefcase. A friend of a friend of mine had a two-hour conversation with Quentin Tarantino himself, and thanks to that talk, I now know the key to the film.*

Remember the first time you were introduced to Marsellus Wallace? The first shot of him was of the back of his head, in the bar as he's talking to Bruce Willis. You'll notice there's a large Band-Aid on the back of his head, as if he'd been operated on.

Now, remember the combination of the lock on the brief-case was 666. Then, remember that when anyone opened the brief-case, it glowed, and they were in amazement at how beautiful it was.

Now, bring in some Bible knowledge, and remember that when the devil takes your soul, he takes it from the back of your head. Yep, you guessed it: Marsellus Wallace had sold his soul to the devil, and was trying to buy it back. The three kids at the beginning of the movie were the devil's helpers. And remember that when the kid came out of the bathroom with a "hand cannon," Jules and Vincent were not harmed by the bullets. "God came down and stopped the bullets," because they were saving a soul. It was divine intervention. Pretty cool, huh?

Pretty cool, indeed. Especially the part about Tarantino graciously taking two hours to explain to a "friend of a friend" the intricacies of *Pulp Fiction* plot points that he hasn't revealed to anyone else! What a guy. Ahem.

As anonymous Internet posting theories go, however, this one isn't bad. Violent, profane, and disturbing as *Pulp Fiction* is at times, there are also a number of religious and spiritual themes infused in the story:

★ Samuel L. Jackson's character, Jules, has a spiritual awakening, and he's forever citing Ezekial 25:17 from the Bible. (The passage Jules recites doesn't exist anywhere in the Bible, but come on, the guy's a hit man, for crying out loud. Give him points for trying.)

★ Uma Thurman snorts a deadly dose of heroin and is literally brought back from the dead after receiving an injection of adrenaline. The Eric Stoltz character who thrusts the needle into her chest and brings her back to life has a hairstyle and beard that makes him resemble the traditional "holy card" images of Jesus.

★ After that volley of bullets mysteriously misses Jules and his partner, Vincent Vega (John Travolta), they have a heated debate about whether it was divine intervention or just plain dumb luck. Note that Jules, who believes it's a sign from God, is saved; Vincent, the eternal skeptic, doesn't survive the film.

It's possible the briefcase contains a human soul—it's possible it contains *anything*, considering that we never see what's inside. But that doesn't explain why anyone who gazes upon the contents recognizes them. I don't know about you, but I have no idea what a human soul looks like. (Maybe it comes with a label.)

In 1994, the *Toronto Star* invited readers to send in their theories on what was in the briefcase. The most popular suggestion was, "an Oscar." Other entries:

- ★ The severed ear from *Reservoir Dogs*.
- ★ O.J. Simpson's other glove.
- ★ A human head.
- ★ The loot from the robbery in *Reservoir Dogs*. (Note: There's a character in *Dogs* named Vic Vega. A relation of Travolta's Vincent Vega in *Pulp Fiction*, perhaps?)

The "winner" was a reader who theorized that the golden aura was a reference to the Robert Aldrich film *Kiss Me Deadly* (1955), in which there's a briefcase that glows because there's a nuclear bomb inside.

Pulp Fiction star John Travolta said in a 1994 interview, "I don't know what's in the case, and Quentin doesn't want us to say even if we think we have an idea. But he does want everyone to have their own interpretation, and I like that.

"Some people say it's the hope of man."

With all due respect, John, the hope of man is that you don't do a sequel to *Battlefield Earth*.

My colleague Roger Ebert tackled the briefcase mystery in a couple of his syndicated "Answer Man" columns, one of which included an explanation from Roger Avary, who, along with Tarantino, won the Academy Award for Best Original Screenplay for their script.

"Originally the briefcase contained diamonds," wrote Avary. "But that just seemed too boring and predictable. So it was decided that the contents of the briefcase were never to be seen. This way each audience member would fill in the 'blank' with their own ultimate contents. All you were supposed to know was that it was 'so beautiful.' No prop master can come up with something bigger than each individual's imagination. At least that was the original idea."

Avary goes on to explain that somebody made the decision to put an orange lightbulb in the briefcase—a decision he calls a "mistake"—which narrowed the mystery item's possibilities to something "supernatural."

Despite the "friend of a friend's" claim that Tarantino has settled the debate, he has never gone on the record with an explanation of the *Pulp Fiction* mystery—probably because there *is* no explanation. It's whatever you want it to be.

Personally, I think it's a miniature tanning bed. That would explain the glow.

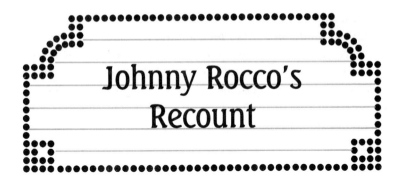

Johnny Rocco's Recount

In the weeks after the wackiest election in the last 100 years of American history, a number of cute little urban legends pertaining to the vote started to sprout in cyberspace. One such story had the 16th century prognosticator known as Nostradamus making this claim in 1555:

Come the millennium, month 12
In the home of the greatest power
The village idiot will come forth
To be acclaimed the leader.

Democrats in particular seemed to delight in passing his message around. To them it was a way of saying, "Okay, we realize we're stuck with this Bush guy, but that doesn't mean he's any smarter than he was last month. Nostradamus had it right!"

The only drawback, and you don't have to be Nostradamus to see this one coming, is that the man never wrote anything like that. (Besides, the "village idiot" in "the home of the greatest power" as we closed out the year 2000 wasn't George W. Bush, it was that guy on the MTV show *Jackass*.) Nostradamus was rarely so specific in his predictions. When he did peer into the future, he would write stuff like:

The year 1999 seven months
From the sky will come the great King of Terror
To resuscitate the great king of the Mongols
Before and after Mars reigns by good luck.

Okay, so that happened. But there's no mention there or in any of the Nostradamus quatrains of a village idiot coming to power, according to the experts who run the various Nostradamus Web sites.

Nor, for that matter, was there any validity to another quotable quote that made the rounds: the claim that Joseph Stalin once said, "It's not the people who vote that count. It's the people [who] count the votes."

As if Stalin ever had to worry about such things.

And then there's my favorite election-related UL: the claim that an Edward G. Robinson monologue from 1948's *Key Largo* was particularly well suited to what was happening during the long recount controversy. The speech was misquoted and/or misinterpreted in a number of newspapers—and of course the erroneous version flew all over the Internet.

According to the half-correct quote, which appeared in *The Boston Globe* and *The New York Times* (and which was later corrected by both newspapers), the gangster Johnny Rocco says, "Let me tell you about Florida politicians. I make them....Then after the election we count the votes, and if they don't turn out right, we recount them and recount them again until they do."

Not quite.

First, the setup. *Key Largo* stars Humphrey Bogart as a war hero who visits the father and the young widow (Lauren Bacall) of an Army pal. (Bogie's character was a "circulation manager for a newspaper" before the war.) The hotel operated by his pal's dad has been taken over by a gang of hoodlums led by Robinson's Johnny Rocco*, a Midwestern gangster with ties to Chicago and Milwaukee who has been in exile in Cuba for the last eight years, but is trying to make a comeback in the Florida Keys.

A nosy deputy gets conked on the head by one of Rocco's boys. After the deputy has regained consciousness, he joins a roomful of people that includes Bogie and Bacall. As Johnny Rocco gets a shave, he addresses the deputy:

You'd give your left eye to nail me, wouldn't you? Yeah. You can see the headlines, can't you? "Local deputy captures Johnny Rocco." Your picture would be in all the papers. You might even get to tell on the newsreel how you pulled it off. Yeah.

Well listen, hick! I was too much for any big-city police force to handle. They tried but they couldn't. Took the United States government to put a rap on me. Yeah, and they couldn't make it stick. You hick! I'll be back pulling strings to get guys elected mayor and governor before you ever get a 10-buck raise.

Yeah, how many of those guys in office owe everything to me. I made them. Yeah, I made 'em, just like a—like a tailor makes a suit of clothes. I take a nobody, see, teach him what to

---

* If you catch *Key Largo* on video or DVD, hit the pause button whenever Johnny Rocco fires his gun and you'll see Robinson flinching and closing his eyes when he pulls the trigger. The actor, who was famous for playing movie toughs, was, in reality, a gentle, sophisticated man of culture who so hated guns that even firing one loaded with blanks would cause him to noticeably recoil.

say, get his name in the paper, pay for his campaign expenses. Dish out a lot of groceries and coal, get my boys to bring the voters out, and then count the votes over and over again till they added up right and he was elected.

Yeah, then what happens? Did he remember when the going got tough, when the heat was on? No, he didn't wanna. All he wanted was to save his own dirty neck....Yeah, 'Public Enemy' he calls me. Me, who gave him his "public" all wrapped up with a fancy bow on it.

In fact, there's no mention whatsoever of "Florida politicians" or "recounts" in the actual screenplay, which was adapted by Richard Brooks and John Huston from a play by Maxwell Anderson.

Who got the idea for the story from Nostradamus, of course.

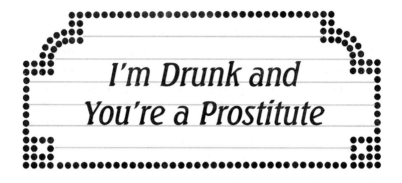

I'm Drunk and You're a Prostitute

Movie titles are like names for rock bands—we've used up most of the good ones, but you have to call your product something, don't you? People can't be expected to pay $8 or $10 for a ticket to something titled, *A Big Fat Stupid Movie We Hope You Like!* (Come to think of it, that's not a bad title. Copyright 2001 by Richard Roeper!)

But even if a movie has a perfectly suitable and quite zingy title in English, what happens when it has to be sold in foreign markets? The translation from English to Spanish or French (or vice versa) can usually be pulled off with little, if any, change in the meaning. But when it comes time to sell a Western movie in the Far East, even some one-word titles would be completely meaningless to the audiences there.

In April of 1998, *The Wall Street Journal*'s Hal Lipper explored this unique problem in an article titled, "Will *Mr. Cat Poop* clean up at the box office in Hong Kong?" Lipper's piece featured an interview with Doinel Wu, "who has spent more than a decade renaming" American films. *Boogie Nights*, for example, was called *His Powerful Device Makes Him Famous*, while *The Full Monty* was known as *Six Naked Pigs,* according to the Mandarin interpretation. *As Good As It Gets* was *Mr. Cat Poop*, and *Nixon* was retitled *The Big Liar*, which just happens to be what I've always called it anyway.

Lipper's article is just the sort of thing at which the *Journal* excels—a clever idea conceived in deadpan fashion that causes editors and writers at other newspapers to grumble about not coming up with the idea, even as they're figuring out a way to quote it or use it as a launching point for their own article on the same subject.

One such newspaper was *The New York Times*. A few months after *The Wall Street Journal* article was published, an article in the *Times*'s "Week in Review" section took a look at the same phenomenon.

The opening anecdote was about the efforts by 20th Century Fox to rename its comedy hit *There's Something About Mary* for foreign audiences. According to the article, *Mary* was titled *Mary At All Costs* in France, *My True Love Will Stand All Outrageous Events* in Thailand, and *Enjoy Yourself in the Game of Love* in Hong Kong.

So far, so accurate. But then the *Times* printed some Hong Kong titles of American and English movies that were so outrageous as to defy belief. Following are some examples.

FROM:	**TO:**
Leaving Las Vegas	*I'm Drunk and You're a Prostitute*
George of the Jungle	*Big Dumb Monkey Man Keeps Whacking Tree with Genitals*
Batman and Robin	*Come to My Cave and Wear This Rubber Codpiece*
Barb Wire	*Delicate Orbs of Womanhood Bigger Than Your Head Can Hurt You*
The Crying Game	*Oh No! My Girlfriend Has a Penis*

★ ★ ★

So much for keeping Hong Kong audiences in suspense with that last title. Apparently nobody over there was to be surprised by the big surprise in *The Crying Game*. If that's the approach, why not just call *The Sixth Sense* something like *The American Psychiatrist Is a Ghost*? (Sorry if I just gave away the big surprise in that movie, but if you hadn't seen it by now, *what were you waiting for*?!?!)

As happens with almost anything of interest that is published in *The New York Times*, juicy nuggets of the article were quoted by many other news organizations—including ABC News, where Peter Jennings closed his broadcast of January 5, 1999, with this comment: "And finally, the new title for *Babe* reminds us that in China the communists are still in charge. *Babe* is now *The Happy Dumpling-to-be Who Talks and Solves Agricultural Problems*."

Nothing like a wacky kicker to end a newscast—even if that wacky kicker is bogus.

This half-legend was created when somebody in cyberspace took a satirical list of Chinese movie titles and attached it to the legitimate article from *The Wall Street Journal.* That's the version that *The New York Times* writer was referencing when he wrote his piece—so he included a bunch of titles that he thought were from a *WSJ* sidebar, when in fact they'd been created by TopFive *(www.topfive.com)*, one of the funnier and more creative humor Web sites on the Internet.

TopFive is a Lettermanesque collection of lists—everything from "Rejected Pokemon Names" to "New State Mottoes" to "Signs Your Cat Is Overweight." In August of 1997, the TopFive people posted a list of 15 Chinese movie titles, compiled by editor Chris White—and nine of those ended up in *The New York Times* piece more than a year later. Even after Howard Kurtz of *The Washington Post* wrote an article about the mix-up, a number of media types kept the bogus title myth alive (for example, the aforementioned Mr. Jennings, who used the *Babe* anecdote a full month after the Kurtz article).

TopFive's White told me he's not surprised but he is "frustrated" that his work has been hijacked in this manner. "There's a 'Wild West' mentality regarding the Internet—that laws don't apply there. I'm constantly amazed that people who should know better fall for this lazy way of thinking....TopFive material has shown up uncredited in [major newspapers and on network TV]—quite often in humor columns. Credit, when given, is usually along the lines of, 'This is from the Internet,' but more often the 'author' fails to mention that the material is from another source, simply stealing TopFive material and passing it off as his/her own.

"More agonizing is the fact that since we started TopFive in 1994, I've received reports from TopFive readers of more than 300 radio stations worldwide [that] have used our material—and 95 percent of them not only fail to give us credit, but they act as if they themselves write the material."

White makes a good point. Whereas the vast majority of journalists and even most radio hosts wouldn't dare lift material verbatim from a book or magazine for fear of a plagiarism suit, there's a different mentality about the Internet—as if we all have an inherent right to pluck material from cyberspace and call it our own.

In the case of the Chinese movie titles, nobody was intentionally deceiving the public; it's just that some really smart people at some really influential news organizations were gullible enough to believe that *Twister* would be retitled *Run! Ruuuuuuuuuun! Cloudzillaaaaaaaaaa!* or that *The Piano* would be called *Ungrateful Adulteress! I Chop Off Your Finger!*

Sure. And I suppose *Titanic* would be *My Beautiful New Boyfriend Is Frozen Dead in the Water!* (Actually, *Titanic* was called, well, *Titanic* in just about every country it was released.)

The TopFive guys were the beneficiaries of a publicity windfall again in the spring of 2000, when Al Gore did a stand-up routine for the Anti-Defamation League that was highlighted by his list of "Jewish and Country Western Songs," including "I Was One of the Chosen People—Until She Chose Somebody Else," "The Second Time She Said 'Shalom,' I Know She Meant Goodbye," and "I've Got My Foot on the Glass, Now Where Are You?"

Nobody thought Gore himself wrote the jokes, but it was assumed that his staff had dreamed up the routine—until news organizations reported that the songs were lifted from the TopFive Web site. Not only that, but Gore wasn't even using the "Top 13 Jewish Country and Western Songs" as compiled by White; he was working from a list of runners-up. The "winners" on the list included "Achy Breaky Hip," "All My Exes Made an Exodus," and "Alright, Already, Enough with the Infidelity!"

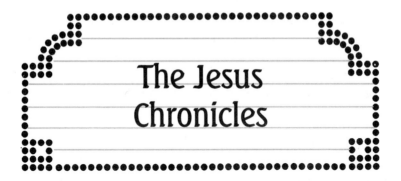

The Jesus Chronicles

Here's a surefire way to get people to sign your petition: include the words *Jesus*, *sex*, and *homosexual* in your pitch letter, in no particular order. From the early 1980s through the mid-1990s, a letter with just such incendiary terms was making the rounds, first via old-fashioned chain mail and later on the Internet.

A popular version:

Modern People News *has revealed plans for a movie based on the SEX LIFE OF JESUS in which Jesus will be portrayed as a SWINGING HOMOSEXUAL! This film will be shot in the U.S.A. this year unless the public outcry is great. Already a French prostitute has been hired to play the part of Mary Magdalene, with whom Christ has a blatant and explicit affair. We CANNOT AFFORD to stand by and DO NOTHING about this disgrace.*

We must not allow this perverted world to drag our Lord through the dirt. PLEASE HELP us to get this film banned from the U.S.A. as it has been in Europe. Let us show how we feel.

Detach and mail the form below to the address shown. Make a few copies and show them to your friends. Only one name per copy!

The attached form letter is usually addressed to an "Attorney General Scott" in Springfield, Ill. (Who knew my home state would be an appropriate setting for a story based on the life of Jesus? Apparently the filmmakers were going to capitalize on the little-known fact that the flatlands of the Midwest look exactly like the land of Galilee!)

Dear Attorney General Scott:

I would like to protest, in the strongest terms possible, the production, filming, and showing of any movie that supposedly depicts the sex life of Jesus Christ. Such a movie would be blasphemous and would be an outrage and contrary to the truth. We urge you to take proper action against this moral corruption.

It's unclear exactly what action the Attorney General of Illinois would be able to take to stop production on such a movie. Military-sounding title notwithstanding, the attorney general of any given state really doesn't have the legal or moral authority to halt production on a movie, or to ban local theaters from showing such a film. (And by the way, if Jesus was gay in this purported movie, why would he be having an explicit affair with Mary Magdalene?)

Nevertheless, hundreds of thousands of outraged Christians signed the petitions and sent them to the state capital—and the volume of letters only increased after a second letter began making the rounds, claiming that "Jimmy Swaggart has reported that the movie in question has been completed, and the movie is scheduled to be shown during the Christmas season, so the time is short to keep this ungodly filth" out of theaters.

Year after year, the warnings continued to spread about the so-called "sex life of Jesus" film, even though no such film was in production and no such film was ever released. (You'd think some of the thousands of folks who signed these petitions would have wondered what happened to the movie. Apparently they forgot about their outrage, or they assumed the signature drive had worked and had driven the demonic film right out of production!) In the meantime, a whole new wave of well-meaning Christians would be signing the same petitions and sending them to the Illinois Attorney General's office, which was so exasperated that it turned to the venerable Ann Landers for help, with a letter of its own (note that the name of the magazine is changed slightly in this letter):

Dear Ann:

The office of the Attorney General of the state of Illinois respectfully requests your assistance in combating an international chain letter that is distressing thousands of Christians and those of other faiths as well. The chain letter is a plea to protest the making of a movie in which Jesus Christ could be depicted as a swinging homosexual. Both our office and the Associated Press have chased down every possible clue and cannot find a shred of truth in the story that such a film was ever in production.

Modern Film News, *which reported the film plans, has been out of business for more than two years. Moreover, 90 percent of the protest mail that has been overwhelming our staff is addressed to the former attorney general, William J. Scott, who has been out of office for more than four years.*

Despite our efforts to get the word to the public that the chain letter is a hoax, we continue to receive approximately 1,000 protests every week and at least a dozen phone inquiries each working day. The inquiries and protests have come from 41 states,

Canada, Puerto Rico, New Zealand, Australia, Cambodia, Spain, Brazil, the Dominican Republic, India, the Philippines, Guatemala, Costa Rica, and Portugal.

We have concluded that the "Jesus movie" rumor originated in 1977 when a suburban Chicago publication, Modern People News, *reported that certain interests in Europe were planning such a film and requested that readers express their opinion of the purported project. The result was the chain letter protest, which, for some unknown reason, has been revived and is sweeping the world.*

We are appealing to you, Ann Landers, to help us get the word out. The scope of your readership and impact on millions of newspaper readers around the world cannot be overestimated. The postage and the phone calls, not to mention the valuable time of employees, run into a great deal of money that could be used for so many worthwhile purposes. Will you please help us?

Neil F. Hartigan, Attorney General, State of Illinois

Landers dutifully printed the letter and urged her readers to ignore the petition, adding: "Hoaxes die hard and the zanier the hoax, the more difficult it is to convince people that it is not true." Good for her, but it's kind of ironic, given that Ann and her twin sister, Abby, have enhanced the veracity of countless urban legends over the years by printing letters from well-meaning readers warning about the "gang initiation of flashing headlights at unsuspecting victims," or the "children who are being abducted at shopping malls," or the "drunk driver who found the body of a little girl pinned to the grill of his car," or "the nude surprise party," among other ULs.

A decade and a half later, the "gay Jesus movie" rumor picked up new steam, courtesy of the Internet. In the fall of 2000, the following e-mail was circulating:

There is a movie coming out in 2001!

Saying that Jesus and his disciples were gay! There is already a play that went on for a while, but never stopped! Maybe we can all do something!

Please send this to ALL your friends to sign to stop the movie from coming out. Already certain areas in Europe have started to ban it from coming to their country and we can stop it too! We just need a lot of signatures and you can help! Please do not delete this! Deleting it will show your lack of faith and a lack of respect for our Lord and Savior Jesus Christ who died for us! Please help!

PLEASE SIGN AND SEND TO EVERYONE YOU KNOW! PLEASE. IF WE WORK TOGETHER WE CAN BAN THIS. PLEASE! To sign this, copy the text and paste it on a new (or forward) message. Then scroll down, sign the bottom and send it on.

Okay, first of all, "send it on" to where? If the e-mail is just forwarded in perpetuity, what entity is going to eventually receive it and actually do something about this rumored film?

Beyond that, might I suggest that unlike some religious leaders, I would never presume to assert what actions would offend the Lord—but something tells me that deleting mass e-mail messages is not a sin that's particularly high on the list. And I hope there's a special place in purgatory reserved for people who author nonsensical sentences such as, "There was already a play for a while but it never stopped!" and punctuate every line with an exclamation point.

There is one bit of truth in the letter, and that's the reference to a play about a homosexual Jesus who has sex with his gay disciples. That was exactly the theme of *Corpus Christi*, a 1998 play from three-time Tony Award winner Terrance McNally that opened at the Manhattan Theater Club in New

York City amidst a swirl of controversy, public demonstrations, protests from Catholic groups, and even bomb threats—though many critics said the only real bomb was onstage.

According to an article in *The Detroit News*, the Manhattan Theater Club's press materials said *Corpus Christi* would be the story of Joshua, who has a "long-running affair with Judas and sexual relations with the other apostles. Only one sexual encounter, a non-explicit one with an HIV-positive street hustler, takes place in any form onstage...If we have offended, so be it. He belongs to us as well as you."

Ticket sales were brisk for the six-week run of *Corpus Christi*, but as of this writing, there are no plans to turn the play into a film—and no indication of whether McNally was inspired to write the play by the long-running urban legend about the gay Jesus movie.

Casa-bunka

It's one of the open secrets of Hollywood: No matter how talented you are or how brightly your star light is shining, from time to time you're going to have to accept a hand-me-down script that's already smudged with someone else's fingerprints. Unless you're at the very top of the A-list—we're talking Tom Cruise, Julia Roberts, Tom Hanks, Jennifer Lopez, Mel Gibson, Jim Carrey—you're probably the second or third choice for a part.

Much of this jockeying for position happens years before principal photography begins. Often the first choice loses interest in a project as the script develops or a new director is signed. Sometimes a scheduling conflict gets in the way. Occasionally it's the filmmakers who come to the realization that they need to go in a different direction.

These factors often work to the advantage of the stars and the movie-loving public. Would *Schindler's List* have been a better film with Kevin Costner in the lead instead of Liam Neeson? Could even the great Marlon Brando have done a more magnificent job than Peter O'Toole in *Lawrence of Arabia*? And isn't Cher glad that Sally Field turned down *Moonstruck*?

Aren't we all grateful that Sylvester Stallone said no to *Coming Home* and the role went to Jon Voight? Can you imagine Meryl Streep and Goldie Hawn as *Thelma and Louise*? Somehow that sounds like a totally different movie.

And to this day, Richard Gere should be sending champagne to John Travolta, who turned down the leads in *American Gigolo* and *An Officer and a Gentleman*.

Years ago, there was a crazy story making the rounds that Groucho Marx was the first choice to play Rhett Butler in *Gone With the Wind*. After being ceaselessly pestered about the casting for the movie, novelist Margaret Mitchell sarcastically told *The New York Times* the part of Rhett should just go to Groucho Marx—but she was kidding. Amazingly, some people took her seriously.

Then, of course, there's *Casablanca*, believed by many to be the most unforgettable romance the cinema has ever known. Who else but Humphrey Bogart and Ingrid Bergman could have played those parts?

Well, Ronald Reagan and Ann Sheridan, according to the Hollywood legend. How many times over the years have you heard that story—especially the part about Ronnie as Rick?

From Molly Haskell of *The New York Times* in May of 1999:

"Think of *Casablanca*, then of Ronald Reagan and Ann Sheridan. Laughable? Nevertheless, they were the original team meant to play the 'We'll always have Paris' lovers, but Warner

Bros. had to settle for Humphrey Bogart and Ingrid Bergman (and Paul Henried in the role originally intended for Dennis Morgan)."

The *Independent* of London, January, 1996:

"When Ronald Reagan turned down the part of Rick in *Casablanca,* he didn't realize that ex-presidents are a dime a dozen, but you can count the number of genuine movie icons—Humphrey Bogart—on one hand."

(Actually, there are probably more movie icons than ex-presidents, but that's another quibble for another day.)

"Bogie wasn't first choice to play Rick," stated the *London Times* in 1998.

Those three examples are but a tiny sampling of the countless newspaper articles that have cited this anecdote as an established part of Hollywood history. The story has been repeated in books and on talk shows, at dinner table conversations and on the radio. Even the most casual fans of *Casablanca* can tell you that it was Ronald Reagan, and not Humphrey Bogart, who was originally slotted to play Rick.

In his dreams, maybe.

Before there was *Casablanca,* there was a play called *Everybody Comes to Rick's*, written by Murray Burnett and Joan Alison. The manuscript of that unproduced play was purchased for $20,000 in 1941 by producer Hal Wallis for Warner Bros., and early casting talk centered on such names as George Raft as Rick and either Hedy Lamarr or Ann Sheridan for Ilsa.

In early 1942, Wallis left Warner Bros. to form his own production company, with *Casablanca* being one of the projects under his umbrella. He signed a deal with Warner Bros. to produce several films for them as an independent contractor who would have creative control—including the casting decisions.

So how did the Reagan legend get started? In January 1942—approximately the same time Wallis was cutting his new deal with Warner Bros.—*The Hollywood Reporter* ran an item, fed to them by a Warner Bros. publicist, saying that Reagan, Ann Sheridan, and Dennis Morgan would star in *Casablanca.* (The item didn't specify which role Reagan would play.) But the decision wasn't up to Warner Bros., it was up to Wallis—and Wallis's first and only choices for the lead roles in *Casablanca* were Humphrey Bogart and Ingrid Bergman. (To lease Bergman's services, Wallis had to cut a check for more than $100,000 to rival producer David O. Selznick, who had her under contract.)

The Hollywood Reporter item was picked up by dozens of newspapers. Within days, however, Warner Bros. was backing away from its own press release, with an announcement that Reagan, Sheridan, and Morgan would be starring in *another* movie. (Sheridan and Morgan—but not Reagan—did go on to co-star in that film, *Wings for the Eagle*.)

Too late. The legend had been born. It doesn't matter that Wallis signed a series of memos in early 1942 indicating that Bogart was his first choice, or that Reagan wouldn't have been available even if he *had* been cast as Rick, due to his status in the Army Reserves and the fact that the studios knew he was almost certain to be called to active duty before *Casablanca* would start filming.

When Reagan was president, he often blurred the line between movie life and reality, whether he was invoking Clint Eastwood's "Make my day" in a challenge to Congress, or relating an anecdote from a war movie as if it really happened. But while Reagan might never have gone out of his way to discourage the *Casablanca* legend, I was also unable to find one instance in the public record where he personally made the claim that he was first choice for the part.

The Curse of
Poltergeist

The 1982 ghostly thriller *Poltergeist* starred Craig T. Nelson and JoBeth Williams as the Freelings, a happily married couple with three children who move into a beautiful home in a new housing development—only to discover that the home is already occupied by nasty-tempered spirits from beyond. Turns out, the housing development was plunked atop a burial ground.

Dominique Dunne played the Freelings' eldest daughter; Oliver Robins was the middle child; and 5-year-old Heather O'Rourke was Carol Ann, the little girl who sees the ghosts in her TV set and is literally sucked through the walls of the house by the angry apparitions.

Poltergeist was such a hit that two sequels were filmed, one in 1986, and one in 1988, but according to the believers of the so-called "curse of *Poltergeist*," the success of the franchise has been shrouded in tragedy. Upon the completion of filming on each movie, one of the young actors has died—a macabre trilogy that started with the death of the oldest child and ended with the death of the little girl who said, "They're heeere!"

Compounding this unspeakable tragedy: Several other actors who appeared in one or more of the *Poltergeist* movies has also died, leaving no room for doubt that there really is a curse.

Or so the story goes.

Sadly, the truth provides plenty of ammunition for the superstitious and the silly who want to believe in things like curses. Oliver Robins is alive and well, but the actresses who played his sisters are gone. Dominique Dunne, the 22-year-old daughter of writer Dominick Dunne, died on November 4, 1982, at Cedars-Sinai Medical Center in Los Angeles. Four days earlier, she had been attacked in the driveway of her home by former boyfriend John Sweeney, who choked Dunne so hard, she fell into a coma from which she never emerged. After being convicted of voluntary manslaughter, Sweeney served less than four years of his six-and-a-half-year sentence and was released from prison in 1986.

On January 31, 1988, Heather O'Rourke, then 12, was experiencing flu-like symptoms. The next day, she collapsed and was taken by helicopter to a hospital in San Diego, but she suffered cardiac arrest and died. It was later determined that Heather had died of septic shock as a result of a bowel obstruction.

The strange and stunning circumstances of Heather's death, which occurred after the filming but prior to the release of *Poltergeist III*, spurred conspiracy theorists and fans of the occult to start talking about a curse. (I've never heard a decent explanation of just who is leveling this curse—ghosts who are unhappy with the way they're portrayed in the movies, perhaps?) Did the deaths of Dunne and O'Rourke, and the fact that *Poltergeist II* supporting players Julian Beck and Will

Sampson had died in the mid-1980s, indicate that this was a pattern?

Of course it wasn't. Beck, who played the spooky preacher who shows up at the Freelings's door in *Poltergeist II*, died of stomach cancer in 1985 at the age of 60. Sampson, best known for his role as the Chief in *One Flew Over the Cuckoo's Nest*, died in 1987, several weeks after receiving an emergency heart–lung transplant. These men died at relatively young ages, but the circumstances of their deaths were not particularly unusual or inexplicable. Beck had been seriously ill for more than a year prior to his passing, and Sampson had undergone the surgery as a last-ditch effort to save his life.

Nor is there anything supernatural or mysterious in regards to the deaths of Dunne and O'Rourke. In fact, it's an insult to attribute their deaths to anything other than the factual circumstances. Heather died because she was afflicted with Crohns' Disease—chronic intestinal inflammation—that led to the complications that induced cardiac arrest. The real tragedy is that her death could have been avoided had the bowel obstruction been detected. In fact, her family won damages in a wrongful death lawsuit against her healthcare provider. And the responsibility for Dunne's death should be placed squarely on the head of the ex-boyfriend who should still be in jail for what he did.

Four actors associated with the *Poltergeist* movies are no longer with us. Two men were ill and passed away; a young woman and a child met with unexpected fates.

FACT OR FICTION?

Tom Green's
Nazi Prank

L ike blowfish, lime-flavored Jell-O, sticking a hot needle in your eye, and walking barefoot over broken glass, Tom Green is an acquired taste, not for everybody. Lacking even an atomic particle of subtle wit or comedic insight, the MTV "funnyman" must resort to loud, stupid, gross-out humor in his desperate quest to get laughs.

Consider Green's cameo as a love interest for his real-life love Drew Barrymore in *Charlie's Angels*, the smash hit adaptation of the old jiggle TV show. Green plays "The Chad," a loser who lives on an old steamboat. His entire shtick consists of talking about himself in the third person ("Why are you leaving? Is it the boat? Is it the Chad?") and falling into the water when he's upset.

Let's put it this way: Bob Denver's interpretation of Gilligan was infinitely more nuanced. Yet the Canadian-born Green (who once earned the ire of many of his countrymen by burning the Canadian flag on TV) is worshipped by millions of teenagers who love his sloppy-weird sense of humor and his fearless quest for a laugh at anyone's expense, including his own. They think he's a genius. I think he's an idiot—but I have to give him credit for his insanely twisted yet brave reaction to testicular cancer surgery in 2000.

Tom Green turned the whole thing into a TV special.

In one of the most grotesquely fascinating television programs in the history of the medium, Green had a film crew follow every excruciatingly explicit detail of his ordeal, from his visits to the doctor to his relationships with friends and family to the surgery itself, which was graphic enough to make even a paramedic lose his appetite. We saw Green getting fitted for a "burial suit," just in case the operation went horribly wrong, and we were allowed to eavesdrop on the "Last Supper" he shared with Barrymore and his parents the night before the surgery.

"Hopefully, I'm not going to die," Green tells the waitress.

"Do you want to see a wine list?" she replies.

The whole thing is so bizarre that when Green makes a joke about it being a hoax, you wonder: Is this an elaborately planned, 21st-century urban legend?

But it isn't. To the tune of the theme song from *St. Elmo's Fire*, the surgeon starts cutting. Weirdly enough, the special winds up being an educational, albeit bizarre, look at one young man's ordeal with testicular cancer.

Given Green's utter lack of an embarrassment gene and his no-sacred-cows approach to comedy, it's not hard to imagine him participating in the shockingly tasteless skit that was described in detail on the Internet in 1999. According to the story making the rounds, Green had dressed up as Hitler and had barged into a Bar Mitzvah, doing a bad imitation of the Führer as the cameras rolled and the horrified guests looked on. (In some versions of the story, Green had done the Hitler routine in a crowded synagogue.)

"This time Tom Green has gone too far!" went one Internet posting. "He filmed the bit without MTV's knowledge, but when they got wind of it, they fired him, confiscated the footage, and burned it. No one will ever see this tasteless, anti-Semitic piece of garbage [that] Green was trying to pass off as 'humor.' Green got what he deserved! Hitler is not funny!"

No, he's not—but making fun of Hitler is a time-honored way of scoring easy laughs, from Charlie Chaplin's *The Great Dictator* to the 1960s TV series *Hogan's Heroes* to Mel Brooks' "Springtime for Hitler" number in *The Producers* to the Hitler/pineapple gag (don't ask if you were fortunate enough to miss it) in the Adam Sandler movie *Little Nicky*.

The problem with Green's supposed bit is that it doesn't mock Hitler—it's a direct assault on a group of Jewish people during a sacred moment of family tradition.

As wacky and offensive as Green might be, and as plausible as it might seem that he would go to such an extreme, the "Hitler at the Bar Mitzvah" story is pure fiction—a new urban legend that appeared out of nowhere and has untraceable roots. (I was unable to uncover a seed of fact that might have grown into the UL, i.e., there's no record of any other comic trying to pull such a stunt, or Green dressing up as Hitler for a sketch on TV.) The story gained such momentum in the winter of 1999–2000 that Green went on the offensive, posting a denial on his Web site:

A message from Tom.

Hey everybody, it's Tom. Listen. All of us at the show here have been reading the message board for the last couple of weeks [and] getting more and more distressed at the persistence and the rate of belief of the rumor that I did a "joke" where I dressed up as Adolf Hitler and did something at a synagogue or at a boy's Bar Mitzvah, or whatever version of this you've heard.

It is so important to me and all of us here at the show for all of the fans to realize that this is a horrible, unfunny rumor, and completely untrue.

It may seem to a lot of people that I'm completely out of control and would do anything to piss people off. This is also untrue. One thing that's so important to me is that if you look, no one on the show ever really gets hurt. They may get riled, but I try never to cross that line to where damage could be done.

I always try to be respectful of people's feelings and beliefs, and the writers and I are always mindful of these things when we are thinking of bits for everyone to laugh at.

Obviously the accompanying rumor that I've been fired by MTV because of this is also not true.

We really hope this message puts this negativity to rest. When you read this, I'd appreciate it if you tell someone who cares.

All right, Peace. Tom.

Green also issued denials in the print and broadcast media:

"It's ridiculous," he said on *Entertainment Tonight* on January 21, 2000. "We don't do that kind of thing."

The Hitler story was also mentioned—and debunked—in feature stories on Green that appeared in the *Los Angeles Times* and in *Time* magazine.

"Contrary to rumor...he did not dress as Hitler to attend a Bar Mitzvah," the *Time* story reported. "Although it is true that he humped a dead moose on camera."

It's interesting that unlike most of his celebrity ancestors who have been prominently mentioned in urban legends, Green didn't just sit by and hope the rumors would die, nor did he buy into the theory that commenting on an urban legend only gives it extra life. He took a proactive role in the UL, using his Web site and the entertainment media to issue strong denials.

Perhaps if Richard Gere had taken a similar approach instead of refusing comment, he would have been able to shake off that gerbil years ago.

INTERESTING NOTE: I was in the audience at *Saturday Night Live* in the fall of 2000 when Green was the host and rumors were rampant that he would marry his real-life love Drew Barrymore on the show. Indeed, Drew and a couple who were identified as Green's parents were there that night. Barrymore even joined Green onstage during his opening monologue and confirmed that they would be getting married at the end of the show—but it was just a gag. As the closing credits rolled, Barrymore was a no-show and the wedding set was struck, while a despondent Green wailed and writhed and cried. Subsequent reports speculated that the wedding was really supposed to take place but that Barrymore had backed out—but from my seat in the bleachers, it seemed obvious that the whole thing was a joke from the start.

Monica Puts Foot in Mouth

When the dust (and God knows what else) had settled from the Clinton–Lewinsky affair, Monica told anyone who would listen that all she wanted to do was fade from the spotlight and regain her privacy.

Right. Her quest for anonymity included interviews with the likes of Stone Phillips and Diane Sawyer on national TV, a book supported by a trans-Atlantic publicity tour, interviews with major magazines, and an endorsement contract with Jenny Craig Weight Loss Programs. What a recluse!

On January 3, 2000, Lewinsky plugged the Jenny Craig deal on CNN's *Larry King Live*, where she uttered what was soon to be called "the first quotable quote of the new century" in e-mails that began circulating almost before the broadcast was over. In response to a question from King about how she had slimmed down, Lewinsky said:

"I've learned not to put things in my mouth that are bad for me."

Talk about a double entendre! The quote was quickly pounced upon by the media here and abroad. A few examples:

James Whitaker in the *London Daily Mirror*: "A quote amused me this week. Monica Lewinsky, asked by chat show host Larry King how she managed to lose so much weight, replied: 'I've learned not to put things in my mouth that are bad for me.' What a disappointment for America's young chaps."

Rob Borsellino in the *Des Moines Register*: "I can't believe this is true, but I can't resist passing along this e-mail I got: Monica Lewinsky on *Larry King* talking about her weight loss—'I've learned not to put things in my mouth that are bad for me.'"

Bill Flick in the *Bloomington* (Ill.) *Pantagraph* under the heading "Today's Quote": "As [spoken] by Monica Lewinsky on *Larry King Live* while discussing her 30-pound weight loss: 'I've learned not to put things in my mouth that are bad for me.'"

The "People" column of Portland's *Oregonian*: "'I've learned not to put things in my mouth that are bad for me.' —Monica Lewinsky."

"Pandora," in the *London Independent*: "The mood of Bill Clinton, said to be suffering from loneliness in the dog-days of his reign, will not have been lifted by the news that an old source of succor has most definitely dried up. Monica Lewinsky, appearing on the CNN *Larry King Live* show, was sharing the success of her latest diet with viewers: 'I have learned not to put things in my mouth that are bad for me,' she confided. Poor Bill, meanwhile, is said to be spending these nights with Buddy, his chocolate-coloured Labradour."

Each of these items ran within three weeks of Lewinsky's appearance on *Larry King Live*. At the same time, the quote was in heavy rotation on the Internet, and my e-mailbox received about a half-dozen messages containing the quote.

I never bought into Lewinsky's innocent victim routine, but in this case I have to rush to her defense—because the quote attributed to her is an absolute fabrication. She never said it on *Larry King Live,* or anywhere else for that matter.

It's true that Lewinsky was King's guest on January 3, 2000, and they did chat about a variety of topics, from Monica's social life to her financial status to the Jenny Craig deal. My favorite snippet focuses on romance:

KING: "Do you intimidate men, do you think? Like guys ask you out—you go out on dates, right?"

LEWINSKY: "Not too many, but—"

KING: "Not too many?"

LEWINSKY: "No."

KING: "You don't get asked out a lot?"

LEWINSKY: "No, not as much as I'd like to. It's difficult. I think it's—"

KING: "For the man?"

LEWINSKY: "I think it's difficult for me and for the guy. It's—I've been lucky that I haven't gone out with a jerk yet."

KING: "No? No nerd?"

LEWINSKY: "But it's—"

KING: "No guy who said, 'What's your sign?'"

LEWINSKY: "Well, they might have, but it was appropriate, so."

KING: "Okay."

First of all, let me state for the record that it is *never* appropriate to ask anyone, not even Monica Lewinsky, "What's your sign?" That wouldn't make you a nerd, it would make you someone who has climbed into a time machine and traveled back to the year 1977. But I have to say that I love that whole exchange. It's like something from a Mamet play about a loopy old uncle asking his niece weird questions at a holiday party.

However, further perusal of the transcript of that show turned up nothing that even remotely resembled the "put things in my mouth" remark. Lewinsky said a number of things that could be categorized as inane or self-serving or just scatter-brained, but she did not say anything that could be construed as an inadvertent or Freudian reference to her liaisons with Mr. Clinton.

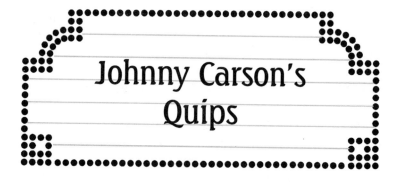

Johnny Carson's Quips

J ohnny Carson was the perfect talk-show host for his era, in no small part because he knew exactly where the line of good taste was—and rather than cross it, he'd just give it a little nudge from time to time.

Carson had an instinctive feel for "adult comedy." If a voluptuous actress was spilling out of her gown, he wouldn't gawk at her like a horny frat boy. He'd raise an eyebrow to the camera in a subtle, conspiratorial manner. If some ditzy starlet left herself wide open for the kill with an inane comment, he'd score with a double-entendre remark instead of going for an easy and somewhat cruel laugh at her expense. Johnny ruled the late-night airwaves at a time when it was an accepted practice for the leering band members to whistle and issue catcalls when some babe sashayed onto the set—but he never tried the jokes Jay Leno and David Letterman routinely get away with every night. He would have been booted from the airwaves faster than you can say "Jack Paar's water closet."

And yet the story of Carson's lurid little exchange with Zsa Zsa Gabor (or Raquel Welch, or Joey Heatherton, or Farrah Fawcett) lives on as an accepted part of *The Tonight Show* history. Most fans believed it happened just as surely as they know Ed Aames once threw a tomahawk that nailed a wooden dummy in the crotch area, and that Johnny once paid a surprise visit to the set of *CPO Sharkey* to berate Don Rickles for breaking his desktop cigarette box, and that Dean Martin once tapped his cigarette ashes into the cup of an unwitting George Gobel, while the audience roared.

The only difference is that while tapes of the Aames and Rickles and Gobel incidents were always trotted out for anniversary shows and can be found on *Best of Carson* video compilations, no record exists of the Zsa Zsa moment—except in the imaginative memories of millions who have convinced themselves that they were watching the show the night it happened.

According to the insistent storytellers, the notorious episode took place in the mid-1960s, when Zsa Zsa was still considered to be something of a sexpot—and enough of a celebrity attraction to be a regular guest on *The Tonight Show*. Upon her introduction, Gabor pranced onto the set in a tight miniskirt and high heels, reveling in the hearty cheers from the male audience members. She was carrying a white Persian cat, which she kept in her lap and stroked with a sensual motion as Carson conducted his interview and pretended to ignore the creature, letting the sexual tension build while the audience tittered and giggled.

Finally, with his impeccable sense of timing, Carson said, "I see you've brought a furry little friend along with you tonight."

"That's right," said Zsa Zsa, as she continued to run her fingers through the cat's luxurious fur. "Would you like to pet my pussy, Johnny?"

Carson waited for the giggles to die down before he dead-panned, "Sure. Move the cat."

Let us now consider the guidelines regarding acceptable behavior and language on network television in the supposedly swingin' 1960s. Married couples on sitcoms slept in separate twin beds. Angry teenagers said, "Gosh darn it!" You couldn't even say "damn" on TV in those days without incurring the wrath of the Federal Communications Commission; in fact, Carson was cited by the FCC in the mid-1960s for a number of slightly risqué comments and sketches that wouldn't make anyone blink in 2001. So even if Gabor had given Johnny such a perfect setup and he had executed the lascivious tip-in, the conversation never would have made it past the network censors.

That's academic, because the incident never happened. None of the books about Carson mention such an incident, nor does Gabor make reference to it in her autobiography. (That Gabor's name has been supplanted over the years by Welch, Heatherton, Fawcett, et al., is further indication that this story is false.)

But what a widespread UL it is! To the point where Jane Fonda (of all people!) broached the subject with Carson in a 1989 *Tonight Show* appearance, by which time the actual words from the apocryphal conversation could be used.

At the time, Zsa Zsa Gabor's name was back in the news because of her arrest for slapping a Beverly Hills motorcycle cop after a traffic stop. Of course, this was great fodder for Carson's monologue, as well as a launching point for Fonda's query.

"You...were talking about Zsa Zsa Gabor earlier," she said. "My son said, 'You know, she was on [*The Tonight Show*] one time. She came there with a cat on her lap and she said to you, 'Do you want to pet my pussy?' And my son said that you said, 'I'd love to if you'd remove the damn cat!' Is it true?"

"No," said Carson. "I think I would recall that."

Almost as famous is the exchange between Carson and Mrs. Arnold Palmer, who told Johnny how she brought her husband good luck: "I always kiss his balls the night before a big tournament."

"I'll bet that makes his putter stand up," replied Johnny.

Sometimes it's Mrs. Jack Nicklaus or Mrs. Tom Watson who feeds Carson the straight line. Could an exchange like that have made it past the censors? Maybe so—though once again, the next time anyone produces a record of that incident will be the *first* time anyone produces a record of that incident. And consider this: Why in the world would *The Tonight Show* book a golfer's wife to be on the show, anyway? Nothing against the spouses of the world's best golfers, but otherwise-unknown significant others have never been in much demand on the network talk-show circuit.

Ah, but what about that time when Burt Reynolds was a guest host on *The Tonight Show* and he gave out a number that people could use to make free long-distance calls? Remember that? Wasn't that great?

See, Reynolds was mad at the phone company because they had screwed him somehow on a bill. So he got his revenge by going on *The Tonight Show* and revealing a super-secret number that could be used to make long-distance calls without getting billed. People who were lucky enough to be watching that night got away with making one call after another, until the phone company realized what was going on and disconnected the special number.

Or so the story goes. Sometimes it's Carson himself who gives out the magic number; more often, it's someone like Reynolds who does it while guest-hosting. In some tellings, the celebrity gives out his own credit card number in a burst of generosity after having won a large settlement in a lawsuit—or he reveals the credit card number of another showbiz personality with whom he's feuding. This version of the urban legend resurfaced in the early 1990s, with Arsenio Hall giving out Eddie Murphy's VISA card number to fans after he and Murphy supposedly had a falling-out over a woman.

The gal in question? None other than Zsa Zsa Gabor.

"Lido Deck, Sir?"

t's one of the most famous stories on Capitol Hill, still repeated to this day even though former actor Fred Grandy hasn't been a congressman since 1994. It seems that when the ex-star of *The Love Boat* arrived in Washington in 1986 after having been elected to the House of Representatives, he was determined to be taken seriously, and he made it clear that he wouldn't tolerate any references to his stint with Captain Stubing and friends. Unfortunately, a congressional page wasn't aware of this policy, and one day when the freshman Iowa congressman stepped into a crowded elevator, the page cracked, "Lido deck, sir?"

Everyone laughed. Everyone except Grandy, that is, who turned crimson red and had the page fired.

Or so the story goes.

This urban legend has dogged Grandy for 15 years, but in a way, he has only himself to blame. First of all, he was on that lame-ass show for all those years, playing that idiot Gopher. If Rob Reiner had been elected to Congress, people in Washington would have been saying, "How's it going, Meathead?" If Jimmie "J.J." Walker had run for office, he would have had to endure cries of "Dynomite!" wherever he campaigned. So it seems only logical that someone would make a *Love Boat* joke from time to time at Gopher's, I mean Grandy's, expense.

Beyond that, it was Grandy himself who gave rise to the legend in speeches that he gave in the late 1980s and early 1990s. Consider the shtick he did for the Washington Press Club in 1987 (the "Ollie" joke is a reference to Oliver North): "It's a thrill for somebody like me to be asked for my opinion. In my old line of work, the only Ollie I knew worked with Kukla and Fran—in fact the only Ollie you know works with Kukla and Fran, too....The House operator still asks me, 'Speaker's lobby or Lido deck?'"

Hey now!

The joke was picked up by a number of publications, including *People* magazine and the *Chicago Tribune*. Little wonder that within a few years, the story was being repeated as fact—with the added twist that Grandy had exploded at the congressional page operating the elevator. In a 1992 article syndicated by Knight-Ridder newspapers, a former page repeated the story and added, "[Grandy] went absolutely crazy. Rumor has it, the page lost his job."

Years later, the "Heard on the Hill" feature in *Roll Call* included a reminder from writer Jim VadeHei of "one of the funniest stories [I] heard upon arriving on Capitol Hill years back. Congressman 'Gopher,' who hated references to his *Love Boat* days, boarded a Capitol Hill elevator years ago, and a wisecracking elevator operator turned to Grandy and deadpanned, 'Lido deck?'

"An intern laughed, but Grandy didn't. The next day the elevator operator was looking for new work, the story goes."

By then, Grandy wasn't telling the joke on himself anymore. In a June, 2000 interview with *The Seattle Times*, he said, "There was a story that haunted me when I first got elected...that once I got on the members' elevator to go up on a vote and there was a page on the elevator and he asked me if I was going to get off at the Lido deck. The apocryphal story is that I had [him] summarily fired and sent back to Muskogee or wherever. First of all, I couldn't have done that even if I'd wanted to. Two, it wasn't true. It was a joke I was telling on myself at the time."

A joke that backfired big time when it turned into a long-lasting urban legend. Fred Grandy is obviously an intelligent man of the world who doesn't deserve to be called "Gopher" anymore, and who should not be remembered in Washington only as the former actor who took himself so seriously that he had a kid fired for making an innocent joke. That said, if you're ever in an elevator someday and the doors open and Mr. Grandy walks in, for my sake, please do it. Please smile brightly and say, "Lido deck, sir?"

Unrelated
Legends

I once asked Shirley MacLaine what she thought of Warren Beatty as a leading man and whether she'd consider playing opposite him in a film. She laughed uproariously and said, "It would be very interesting to co-star with Warren, though I don't think a love scene would be a great idea!"

Probably not, seeing as how MacLaine and Beatty are brother and sister.

We know that, but we kinda forget it from time to time, don't we? Warren and Shirley look nothing like each other, and they're rarely seen together, and they seem to be from different worlds—Warren being a citizen of the planet Earth, and Shirley hailing from her own special galaxy. It's hard to picture them growing up as siblings.

Not that MacLaine and Beatty are the only "surprising" relatives in Hollywood. Consider these other interesting celebrity combos with blood ties:

★ Larry Hagman of *I Dream of Jeannie* and *Dallas* fame is the son of Mary Martin, best known for playing Peter Pan on Broadway.

★ Wacky, tattoo-spangled, Academy Award-winning actress Angelina Jolie is the daughter of Academy Award-winning actor Jon Voight. (He played the coach in *Varsity Blues*, for you kids out there.)

★ Comic genius Albert Brooks (real name Albert Einstein, if you can believe it) is the brother of Super Dave Osborne, real name Bob Einstein. And their father was beloved radio comic Harry "Parkyakarkus" Einstein.

★ Mia Farrow is the daughter of the late Maureen O'Sullivan.

★ Actress Talia Shire (Adrian in the *Rocky* films) is the sister of director Francis Ford Coppola, who, of course, oversaw her performance as Connie Corleone in the *Godfather* flicks.

★ Nicolas Cage is Coppola's nephew. In fact, Cage used his given name of Nicolas Coppola in the credits for *Fast Times at Ridgemont High*, in which he has a tiny role.

★ Actress Dina Merrill's father was E.F. Hutton. When he talked, she presumably listened.

★ Piano-pounding wild man Jerry Lee Lewis is the first cousin of remorseful televangelist Jimmy Swaggart.

★ Carrie "Princess Leia" Fisher is the daughter of Debbie Reynolds and Eddie Fisher.

- ★ Richard Patrick, the lead singer in the band Filter ("Take My Picture"), is the brother of Robert Patrick, who was in *Terminator 2* and is now in *The X-Files*.
- ★ Actress Blythe Danner's daughter is Gwyneth Paltrow.
- ★ Melanie Griffith is the daughter of Tippi *The Birds* Hedren.
- ★ Actress Ann Baxter was the granddaughter of famed architect Frank Lloyd Wright.
- ★ Actress Natasha Gregson Wagner is the daughter of Natalie Wood.

Then there are the celebrities who are related not by blood or marriage, but by urban legend. They're often linked because of a passing physical resemblance, or because someone made a joke that was taken seriously—and all it takes is one posting on the Internet for that misunderstood joke to become an accepted part of Hollywood lore.

The story that Phyllis Diller is Susan Lucci's mom, and that Lucci and fellow soap opera actress Robin Strasser are sisters, started making the rounds in the late 1980s and picked up steam again a decade later. Lucci began playing Erica Kane on the ABC-TV soap *All My Children* in 1970 and she racked up something like 624 daytime Emmy nominations before finally winning one of the damn things in 1999. She is an attractive, diminutive woman with chestnut hair and sharp facial features—as is Strasser, who stars on another ABC-TV soap, *One Life to Live*.

Lucci was born December 23, 1948, in Westchester, N.Y.; Strasser entered the world on May 7, 1945, in the Bronx. Certainly Strasser and Lucci could play sisters (sisters who are in love with the same man, who's dying of a terminal illness and has a mysterious secret!) in a made-for-TV weeper.

But could Phyllis Diller be the mother of these two divas? There actually is more than a hint of a physical resemblance between the wacky Diller and the melodramatic "sisters" Strasser and Lucci. As of this writing, Diller is 83, Strasser is 55, and Lucci is 52, so it's chronologically possible.

Yet nobody is related to anybody in this scenario. Diller was a 37-year-old mother of five when she launched her performing career, perfecting the domestic goddess routine decades before Roseanne followed a similar path. But neither Strasser nor Lucci are among the five kids Diller had with husband Sherwood (forever immortalized as "Fang" in her old routines). Nor are Strasser and Lucci related to one another.

It's easy to see how Lucci and Strasser could be linked— they're soap opera stars a few years apart, who look like each other. Simple. But my guess is that the Lucci–Diller UL was hatched by someone who thought it would be funny (in a slightly mean kind of way) to start the rumor that the aging soap queen was, in fact, the daughter of someone who deliberately "uglied" herself up and made her plain appearance a cornerstone of her comedy routines.

Neil Diamond sure must be proud. He has not one, but two, famous sons—Mike D (full name Mike Diamond) of the Beastie Boys, and actor Dustin Diamond, best known for playing Screech for all those years on *Saved by the Bell*.

Or so the UL goes. The idea of Mr. "Song Sung Blue" fathering one of the rowdy Beastie Boys is pretty funny—oh for a duet of "You Don't Bring Me Flowers" or "Forever in Blue Jeans"!—but it's not true. Nor is the "Love on the Rocks" man the paternal figure in the life of Dustin Diamond, although, once again, the idea of Screech joining his glitter-outfitted father onstage in Vegas is a hoot.

Incidentally, Neil Diamond's real name is...Neil Diamond. Some biographies list Diamond's birth name as Noah Kaminsky, but the singer was born with the name of Neil Leslie Diamond in Brooklyn, N.Y., on January 24, 1941. His birth records and high school yearbooks confirm that he has always gone by the name of Neil Diamond.

The "Noah Kaminsky" story was the inadvertent creation of Diamond himself, who told *The New York Times* and Barbara Walters in interviews several years apart that he had seriously considered changing his name to that moniker. (Diamond has also said he thought about going with a stage name of "Ice Cherry" or "Eice Cherry.")

For the record: Neil Diamond sang "Cherry, Cherry," but he was never named "Ice Cherry" or "Noah Kaminsky." He has four children, including two sons, but their names are Jesse and Micah, and neither one has ever been a Beastie Boy or an annoying actor on a campy-corny TV show.

Was Lucy
a Commie?

"Luuuuuuuuuucy! You got some 'splainin' to do!"

Desi Arnaz wasn't the only one bellowing that catch phrase back in the 1950s. The FBI and the dreaded House Un-American Activities Committee (HUAC) essentially were saying the same thing to the flame-haired comedienne Lucille Ball in 1953, as they asked the musical question, "Are Lucy's politics a deeper shade of red than her hair?"

Don't laugh. Well, go ahead and laugh, but let's not forget that in the early 1950s, the likes of J. Edgar Hoover and Sen. Joseph McCarthy and his witch-hunting henchmen rocked Hollywood—ruining careers, decimating friendships, breaking loyalties, and destroying lives by casting a wide-ranging net of suspicion over any actor, writer, producer, or director who had displayed even the slightest inclination toward Communist activities. You didn't have to be a card-carrying member of the Party to attract the government's scent; all it took was the scent of Communist ties. If you had once attended a meeting or two out of curiosity, or if you were associated with someone who was a known Commie, you, too, could be painted and tainted red.

I Love Lucy premiered on CBS on October 15, 1951, with an episode that had the not-exactly-cryptic title "The Girls Want to Go to a Nightclub." (It was the Mertzes' 18th anniversary. Fred and Ricky wanted to go to the fights; Ethel and Lucy wanted to party the night away at the Copacabana. Hilarity ensued.) By May of the following year, *I Love Lucy* was far and away the most popular series on TV, with an estimated 11 million homes tuning in every Monday night—an astounding figure when you consider that there were only 15 million television sets in the entire country at the time. Not only was *I Love Lucy* a huge hit, it was a groundbreaking show on many levels, from the technique of multiple-camera filming in front of a live studio audience to the controversial showcasing of Lucy's pregnancy to television's first rerun, the rebroadcast of an episode titled "The Diet," in 1952.

But in 1953, there was a black cloud hovering over all of this fantastic success, as whispered rumors about Lucy's Communist affiliation had escalated into a full-fledged controversy. Ball had reportedly registered to vote in 1936, when she was 24, and had listed her political affiliation as the Communist Party. Private citizens were writing letters to the FBI, asking about the rumors of Lucy and/or Desi being card-carrying members of the Communist Party. Tipped off about these stories, the National Heart Association reneged on its plans to name Lucy and Desi as "Mr. and Mrs. Heart, 1953."

In the meantime, the FBI was compiling an extensive file on Ball. (The 142-page file, with some entries and passages blacked out, is available under the Freedom of Information Act. The transcripts and excerpts quoted hereafter are contained in that file.)

Selected passages from the FBI report:

Records of the Registrar for Voters of Los Angeles County, Los Angeles, California, reflected that [name deleted] and Lucille Ball, 1334 North Ogden Drive, Los Angeles, California, registered to vote as Communists on March 19, 1936....

Rita N. Vale, a Hollywood writer and admitted former Communist Party member in Los Angeles, California, furnished a sworn deposition [on July 22, 1940, stating that]...in 1937 that she attended a Communist Party new members' class at the home of actress Lucille Ball. Vale stated that Ball was not present at the meeting but that the person in charge (unidentified) specifically stated that Ball knew the character of the meeting and approved of it taking place in her home.

The Daily Worker *issue of April 10, 1951, contained an article captioned, "Where are the Big Stars Who Once Opposed the un-American."...Among those Hollywood personalities named as previously being opposed to the HUAC was Lucille Ball...Lucille Ball...signed [a] certificate as a sponsor for Emil Freed, a Communist Party candidate for Assembly, 57th District in 1936; that Lucille Ball was appointed [to] the State Central Committee of the Communist Party of California, in 1936....*

To put this in perspective, one has to appreciate just how wildly popular Lucy was in the early 1950s, and just how much the Communist Party was loathed and feared. It would be as if somebody unearthed documents in the 1990s showing that Jerry Seinfeld had supported Saddam Hussein!

Lucy found herself in this pickle because of her grandfather's Socialist leanings. Her father died when she was just 4, and her mother remarried a roustabout who had a drinking and gambling problem, so she and her brother were sent to live with her grandparents. In fact, Lucy referred to her grandfather, Fred Hunt, as "Daddy." Hunt was much loved by Lucy and her brother—so much so that when she registered to vote at the age of 24, she (and presumably her brother) listed herself as a member of the Communist Party, "to make an old man" happy, as she later put it. That Lucy was listed as a delegate for the Party, that her house was used for meetings, that her name was signed to documents confirming her affiliation—this was all news to her, according to her testimony in front of the House Un-American Activities Committee on September 4, 1953.

Selected excerpts from investigator William Wheeler's questioning of America's most beloved comic actress:

WHEELER: "You did register to vote [in 1936] as a Communist or intending to vote the Communist Party ticket?"

BALL: "Yes."

WHEELER: "Would you go into detail and explain the background, the reason you voted or registered to vote, as a Communist or person who intended to affiliate with the Communist Party?"

BALL: "It was over our grandfather, Fred Hunt. He just wanted us to, and we wanted to please him. I didn't intend to vote that way. As I recall, I didn't. My grandfather started years ago. He was a Socialist, as long as I can remember. He is the only father we ever knew, my grandfather. My father died when I was tiny, before my brother was born...."

WHEELER: "Have you ever been a member of the Communist Party?"

BALL: "No."

WHEELER: "Have you ever been asked to become a member of the Communist Party?"

BALL: "No."

WHEELER: "Did you ever attend any meetings that you later discovered to be Communist Party meetings?"

BALL: "No."

★ ★ ★

WHEELER: "Are you aware that you were a member of the Central Committee of the Communist Party for the year 1936?"

BALL: "Was I aware before you told me, you mean?"

WHEELER: "Yes."

BALL: "No."

(NOTE: Wheeler then produced a document showing Ball to be one of three delegates to the Central Party Committee, as named by Emil Freed, and asked Ball to explain her signature on the document.)

BALL: "I have no explanation. I haven't signed it. I don't know where it came from, or what. My name is misspelled. The address is right, that's all."

★ ★ ★

At the conclusion of the Q-and-A session, Ball was asked if she had anything she wanted to add. She noted that she did something that "wasn't wrong" in 1936 but apparently was wrong according to the climate of the 1950s, and added:

"I have never done anything for Communists, to my knowledge, at any time. I have never contributed money or attended a meeting or even had anything to do with people connected with it...I am not a Communist now. I never have been. I never wanted to be. Nothing in the world would ever change my mind.

"It sounds a little weak and corny now, but at the time it was very important because we knew we weren't going to have

Daddy with us very long. If it made him happy, it was important at the time. But I was always conscious of the fact that I could go just so far to make him happy. In those days...it was almost as terrible to be a Republican [as it was to be a Communist]...."

The testimony was not televised, and news of Ball's appearance before the Committee did not immediately surface—but within a week, it was splashed all over the news. On September 12, 1953, Arnaz addressed the studio audience that had assembled for a filming of the first episode of the new season:

"Before we go on, I want to talk to you about something serious," he said. "We all know what it is. The papers have been full of it all day.

"Lucille is no Communist! Lucille has never been a Communist, not now and never will be. I was kicked out of Cuba because of Communism. We both despise the Communists and everything they stand for!

"I was very anxious for all of this to come out. I know that you would find the truth, that Lucy had nothing to do with this and she's completely clear. We both despise anything and everything that smacks of Communism."

In the midst of the controversy, Lucy and Desi also took a phone call from the all-powerful, all-knowing Hedda Hopper, who recounted their conversation in her column in the *Los Angeles Times*, quoting Lucy as saying, "It is true that I talked to a representative of the Un-American Activities Committee, and gave full, truthful answers to all his questions. I am very happy to have had this opportunity to reply to all the unfounded rumors and hope that the committee will release a full transcript of the information I gave them."

Hopper reported that Desi then got on the phone and said, "You tell your readers this, Hedda. The only thing that is red about this kid is her hair—and even that is not legitimately red. We are in the clear all the way."

Although Rep. Donald Jackson of the HUAC uttered the chilling words, "No case is ever closed," the controversy pretty much died with Ball's straightforward testimony, the strong denials that she and Desi issued, and the government's findings that after registering as a Communist in 1936, Lucy never once voted Commie and didn't participate in any subversive activities from that point on. Major sponsors of *I Love Lucy* voiced their support, the ratings didn't suffer at all, and the show flourished for several years.

In other words, Lucy really did do it for dear old (grand)daddy. Despite persistent rumors that live on to this day, Lucille Ball was never a card-carrying member of the Communist Party.

Mean
Martha Stewart

When I started doing various media jobs that placed me in the public eye, I made a vow to never utter the words, "Don't you know who I am?" It's a terribly off-putting thing for a national celebrity, or a local celebrity, or a near-celebrity, or someone-who-mistakenly-thinks-he's-a-celebrity, to say to another human being.

First of all, who cares. Unless you're Jesus Christ and you've come back to Earth to straighten out this whole mess, you shouldn't be so full of yourself that you're bellowing, "Don't you know who I am?" to people. More to the point, if you find yourself in a circumstance where you have to ask that question, it's already been answered for you! Either the person you're addressing obviously doesn't know who you are, or she is fully aware of your celebrity and she's still choosing to treat you in such a manner that has you asking that egotistical question. What she's saying is: "Yeah, so you're on some stupid sitcom. It's still not going to get you on a flight that's overbooked...."

Consider what happened to Martha Stewart as a lesson.

The legendary goddess of potpourri has an estate on Mount Desert Island in Maine, and one day she was waiting in a long line at the local market when she asked the clerk if she could use their telephone.

"Sorry," the clerk said. "We're not allowed to let customers tie up the phone. Company rules."

Steam shot out of Martha's ears as she said, "DON'T YOU KNOW WHO I AM?"

"Nope," said the clerk. "I don't."

"I can't believe this!"

At that point the gentleman behind Stewart gently tapped her on the shoulder. She whirled around with fire in her eyes and said, "What!?"

"Madame, do you know who I am?"

"I have no idea," said Stewart.

"Well, my name is David Rockefeller, and they won't let me use the phone either."

You gotta love the mental image of the self-aggrandizing maven of arts and crafts getting her comeuppance in such a public way. To quote Martha, "It's a good thing."

But not a true thing. Stewart has a reputation for being a demanding taskmaster with a gigantic ego, and there are enough stories about her allegedly insufferable behavior to fill a number of magazine articles and a couple of books—literally. And she has been involved in a number of documented and alleged incidents that aren't exactly in keeping with a hearth-and-home image, from her nasty divorce to an ugly feud with an East Hampton's neighbor to stories about her mistreating employees and having a vocabulary that would make a truck driver blush.

The market incident, however, seems to be entirely fictitious. From the September 2, 2000, edition of *The Boston Globe*:

"'It's a nice little story, but it didn't happen,' says Anne Tucker, manager of the Village Market in Seal Harbor on Mount Desert Island, where the encounter probably would have occurred. Tucker has heard the story a zillion times, and says it doesn't ring true: 'First off, David Rockefeller would never announce himself that way.'"

Another Martha-related UL claims that she is a terrible cook and an extremely uncoordinated individual who couldn't bake or create any of her signature creations if her life depended on it. According to this UL, Stewart has staff members who do all of her cooking, even in her home kitchen when she's throwing parties. And when she's crafting something on TV, those are another woman's hands you see whenever there's a close-up. (Hey, didn't George Costanza do some hand-modeling work on *Seinfeld*?)

Then there are the stories about Stewart backing out of her driveway and running over the neighbor's dog (or cat), killing the poor animal. Martha's supposed reaction? She sues the pet's owner to recover damages sustained to the back bumper of her fancy SUV.

We stress here that NONE of the aforementioned stories about Stewart is backed by hard evidence. No doubt these vindictive, fictitious tales thrive because there are so many people who loathe Stewart and the billion-dollar empire she has built on the neuroses of upwardly mobile women who think they're failures if they're not Hillary Clinton in the workplace and Betty Crocker at home. The Martha Stewart ULs either embarrass her or reveal her to be a fraud, thus comforting those who are overwhelmed and intimidated by this woman's ferociously obsessed way of life.

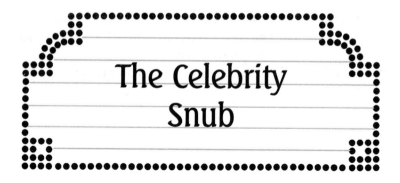

The Celebrity Snub

Whenever I feel the urge to belittle or mock someone who has just told me a "true story" about someone famous—a story that I know to be nothing but a 100 percent, genuinely recycled urban legend—I try to remember that I've been there too. I, too, have happily swallowed many a Hollywood-based UL as a nutritious nugget of truth that I've gleefully repeated over the years as an example of my pop culture history pedigree—only to one day hear a strangely similar story in a slightly different form, or with different names in the "starring" roles. And then, suddenly, I'd realize that for all that time, I'd been unwittingly contributing to the myth-making machinery.

I blame it all on Dad.

My father is one of the all-time great skeptics—he regularly marks the newspaper with scoffing remarks or informed questions regarding a dubious assertion he sees in a story—and he's been an urban myth aficionado for a couple of decades, but that doesn't make him immune to the lure of the well-formed UL about some famous face. It was Dad who first told me the story of the Celebrity Snub. Most likely, he recounted the tale one night in the 1970s when we were in the living room watching *The Tonight Show Starring Johnny Carson*, with Don Rickles making one of his frequent appearances.

Rickles, of course, is the frog-faced comedian who made it big on the strength of his equal opportunity insult routine, in which he would lambaste every ethnic group from Native Americans to gays to African-Americans to Italians, trafficking in broad and easy stereotypes, yet somehow managing to stop just short of being truly offensive. Rickles also had no qualms about harpooning his fellow celebrities, whether he was mercilessly ribbing Ed McMahon about guzzling too many beers with his Clydesdale friends or harassing Carson about his numerous ex-wives. In fact, Rickles was so fearless and funny that he was the only guy in Hollywood who could get away with making jokes about Frank Sinatra—and he could even pull off a practical joke at the Chairman of the Board's expense, or so the story goes.

One day back in the early 1960s, at the height of the Rat Pack craze, Rickles was having dinner with an impressionable starlet at a Las Vegas restaurant when he caught a glimpse of Sinatra and his entourage making their way through the casino. The comedian made an excuse about needing to use the bathroom and then hustled after Frank. He caught up to him at the bar, where he kissed his ring and made a few jokes for everyone's amusement before whispering a humble request into the Chairman's ear.

"Listen, can you do me a big favor?" said the sweaty little comic. "I've got this great-looking dolly in the restaurant and I'm trying to cash my chips with her, if you know what I mean, but she's playing hard to get. If you could just come by the table for half a minute to say hello, I know that would impress the hell out of her and she'd be mine tonight."

Ever the gracious don, Sinatra agreed to help out a friend.

"Great!" said Rickles. "You're the best, Frank. If you could just wait a few minutes and then come by, I'd be forever in your debt."

Rickles returned to his date just as their meals were arriving, and he resumed their conversation as if nothing had happened.

A few minutes later, the restaurant buzzed with excitement as Sinatra himself entered and headed straight for Rickles's table.

"Don!" he said with exaggerated excitement, his arms open. "Had I known you were here I would have sent over champagne. How are you, my friend?"

The starlet's jaw dropped to her cleavage, but Rickles didn't even look up from his dinner.

"Not now, Frank," he said with a dismissive wave of his hand. "Can't you see I'm eating?"

In my eagerness to believe that Rickles had the moxie to pull off such a stunt, I never considered what might have transpired in the moments immediately after Rickles' zinger. Hard to picture Sinatra skulking away like a schoolchild who had been scolded, isn't it? More likely he would have poured a highball on Rickles's head, or stolen the starlet from his grasp with a snap of his fingers, just to teach him a lesson. Of course, then the story wouldn't be so funny, would it?

But the best evidence that this incident never took place is its resurgence in recent years, as a first-person anecdote circulating on the Internet, with celebrities ranging from Michael Jordan to Bill Gates getting set up by lesser lights—or by total strangers.

Here's a version that was sent to me:

My name is Chris Franklin and I've always believed in the aggressive approach, in life and especially in business. Here's a true story. I was in the Admirals' Club at the airport last week when I spotted none other than Bill Gates, quietly tapping away on his laptop in a corner by himself. As it so happens, I was schmoozing with an important client before we were getting on a flight to Seattle, so when my client went to the bathroom, I dashed over to Gates, introduced myself as his biggest fan, and asked him if he'd make my year with a simple favor. All he had to do was come over and pretend to know me, and I'd look like a total bigshot.

He agreed. A few minutes later I was talking to my client when Gates tapped me on the shoulder and said, "Chris, it's great to see you!"

And I replied: "Not now, Gates. Can't you see I'm busy?!"

Uh-huh. And then Don Rickles walked by and said, "Quit stealing my story, you hockey puck!"

MUSIC

Madonna,
Tip-Top Starlet

According to the old joke, satire is what closes on Saturday night. That may still hold true. But in the new age of instant misinformation, satire is also what gets reproduced as a straight news story on the Internet and is then picked up by mainstream news organizations, thus completing the circle and giving the satirical piece of work a veneer of credibility it does not merit.

Case in point, Madonna's "Hungarian" interview.

In 1996, Madonna was interviewed by a reporter for the Hungarian newspaper *Blikk* while she was in Budapest filming *Evita*. Because Madonna does not speak Hungarian, and the reporter did not speak English, an interpreter was needed to relay the questions back and forth.

The interview ran on the front page of the May 2, 1996, edition of *Blikk*, under the headline, "Madonna Visszater," which means, "Madonna is Returning." In a clever and funny piece about the story, Karen Thomas of *USA Today* had Madonna's answers, which had originated in English but had been translated to Hungarian, translated back again to English. This was no easy trick, as Hungarian is an exceedingly difficult language and is not particularly compatible with English—but it made for some chuckles. By the time Madonna's remarks had been through the interpretation blender several times, something had definitely been mangled, if not lost, in the translation.

Asked about her pregnancy, Madonna said, "I'm not an experimental object," and added, "The conception is symbolical. I feel that both my pregnancy and the film itself are basically change my life."

Even George W. Bush makes more sense than that!

As for her favorite Hungarian restaurant, Madonna was quoted as saying, "I was unable to take any special gastronomic excursions."

She also complimented Hungarian men for their looks but added, "These are, of course, generalities, however I am a person of prompt decision."

Finally, Madonna said it was indeed possible for "an unapproachable star" to get "close to a very everyday person. This is the caprice of love."

As Dana Carvey imitating Johnny Carson would say, "Now that is some weird stuff. Some weird and wacky stuff."

Witty as it might have been, the *USA Today* article didn't attract much attention after it ran—but it did light the fires of inspiration of Garry Trudeau, the creator of the *Doonesbury* comic strip and an occasional essayist. In the May 20, 1996, issue of *Time* magazine, Trudeau published a piece titled, "'I am a Tip-Top Starlet'; In Which Something is Lost, But Much is Gained, in the Translation." He started the column by re-capping Madonna's visit to Budapest and the interview she gave to *Blikk*, and then he mentioned that "at the request of *USA Today*, Madonna's comments were then translated from Hungarian back to English for the benefit of that paper's readers. To say that something was lost in the process is to be wildly ungrateful for all that was gained...*USA Today*, presumably pressed for space, published only a few of [Madonna's] gems, leaving the rest to the imagination, whence has sprung the following complete transcript[.]"

You'll note that Trudeau tells the readers up front that the article to follow is the product of his imagination. His made-up, fictional, not real interview contains passages that make the reporter and Madonna sound as if they're imitating the "Wild and Crazy Guys" characters from *Saturday Night Live*.

> *BLIKK*: "Madonna, Budapest says hello with arms that are spread-eagled. Did you have a visit here that was agreeable? Are you in good odor? You are the biggest fan of our young people who hear your musical productions and like to move their bodies in response."
>
> MADONNA: "Thank you for saying these compliments. [Holds up hands.] Please stop with taking sensationalist photographs until I have removed my garments for all to see [laughs]. This a joke I have made."

Chuckle-inducing, to be sure. But completely fictitious. One hint of the interview's bogus quality: The interviewer's questions are just as mangled as Madonna's answers. (Another sample question: "Are you a bold hussy-faced woman that feasts on men who are tops?") This makes no sense if the interview is supposed to be real. Why would the Hungarian interviewer's syntax be so disjointed? He's asking the questions in his native tongue! Nevertheless, portions of Trudeau's hilarious piece were cut and pasted all over the Internet—and suddenly the *USA Today* article and the satirical takeoff were joined like Siamese twins. Columnists, editors, and reporters across the country jumped on the Trudeau essay and festooned it with credibility.

On May 16, 1996, the *Charlotte News and Observer* reported:

"When Madonna granted an interview to a Budapest publication recently, she had no idea what she was getting into. The Material Girl was in Hungary filming *Evita* when she talked with the newspaper *Blikk*. It went thus: The paper asked a question in Hungarian, then it was translated into English for Madonna, then the answer was translated into Hungarian for *Blikk*. Madonna's response was translated into English at *USA Today*'s behest. The result was a comedy of errors. A sample:

"*BLIKK*: 'Madonna, Budapest says hello with arms that are spread-eagled. Did you have a visit here that was agreeable? Are you in good odor?'

"MADONNA: 'Thank for you for saying these compliments. [Holds up hands.] Please stop with taking sensationalist photographs until I have removed my garments for all to see [laughs]. This is a joke I have made.'"

Hmmm, sound familiar? (Although it's interesting to note that a portion of Trudeau's set-up question got lost in the translation from satirical piece to budding urban legend.) All of the questions and answers in the *News and Observer* article are lifted from the *Time* essay rather than the *USA Today* article.

The *London Daily Mail*, the *St. Louis Post-Dispatch*, the *Asheville* (N.C.) *Citizen-Times*, the *Tampa Tribune,* and a number of newspapers in the Knight-Ridder chain also were victims of the mix-up; they unwittingly went with the fictional

"hussy-woman" questions rather than any of the real transla-
tions. Two years later, the confusion still reigned, as evidenced
by an article in the August 14, 1998, edition of the *London
Daily Guardian* that noted the Internet popularity of the Madonna interview, but failed to point out that it was originally
published as a comedy bit.

From the *Guardian* article: "When *Time* magazine reproduced this journalistic gem, it commented, 'To say that something was lost in the process is to be wildly ungrateful for all
that was gained.'"

Yes, and to get the facts that jumbled is to further propa-
gate an urban legend.

Let It Bleed

For all their strutting and posing and swearing and posturing onstage, today's young rockers and rappers often seem like kiddies playing dress-up compared to their musical ancestors from the 1960s and 1970s. Keith Moon destroying his drum kit, Janis Joplin swigging Jack Daniel's onstage, Jimi Hendrix setting fire to his guitar, Jim Morrison unzipping to expose his innermost insecurities—now those were the days of true debauchery!

The onstage, backstage, and hotel room excesses of those Rock and Roll Hall of Famers are well documented—and at times quite exaggerated. For every true story about a guitarist destroying his hotel suite with a chain saw or a groupie making plaster casts from the genitalia of her conquests, there's an apocryphal tale about animals being executed onstage or male rock stars engaging in trysts with each other.

One of the more enduring (and disgusting) rock ULs is the story of the preening star who collapses onstage and is rushed to the hospital—where a "quart of semen" is pumped from his stomach just in time to save his life. (Rod Stewart and Elton John are the names most often attached to this legend.) When I was in college, one of my roommates ridiculed me for buying tickets to a Rod Stewart concert, saying he hoped Stewart didn't have another onstage collapse. When I told him I had no idea what he was talking about, he related the UL and said, "I can't believe you didn't know that story. I thought you were up on stuff like that."

In my defense, I had yet to receive my postgraduate degree in Urban Legendology, so I didn't immediately recognize the tale as a UL—but I was sure the story had to be total bunk. The ridiculously huge amount of body fluid in question and the realities of the human digestive system are just two clues to the bogus nature of the tale, not to mention that if one of the world's biggest pop stars had experienced such an astonishing collapse in a public venue in front of 20,000 adoring fans, something tells me it might have made the papers. Usually aimed at sexually androgynous rockers, the stomach-pumping UL is born from homophobia and jealousy; it's a way for sexually threatened straight males to lash out at the "little queer" who has all those gals screaming as he prances about in his tights and his poofed-up hair and his velvet boots.

Another strange sexual UL involves Mick Jagger, Marianne Faithful, and a strategically placed Mars bar. Suffice to say, it never happened.

Other rock ULs are half-truth cocktails, concocted from a blend of onstage theatrics, wild exaggerations, and pure lies. Frank Zappa's uniquely bizarre sense of humor led to some gross and shocking behavior in concert—but he never did anything involving human feces, contrary to popular lore. Alice Cooper used pints of fake blood, snakes, and a magician's guillotine in his concert appearances, but he never harmed himself or any of God's creatures. Marilyn Manson has been accused of committing any number of atrocities onstage—everything from throwing puppies into the crowd and refusing to keep playing until they're killed to defecating onstage and demanding a fan ingest the waste—but he's no more violent than Cooper was 25 years ago. It's an act, people.

What about Ozzy Osbourne and his tendency to munch on bats? According to Osbourne, it did happen—but it wasn't a regular part of his act, nor was it even a planned event. It happened exactly once, at a 1982 concert in Des Moines, Iowa, when a fan tossed a live bat onstage. (How this fan managed to bring in a live bat and keep it under his jacket or shirt is beyond me.) Osbourne picked it up, thinking the thing was a toy, and he took a bite.

"No matter what achievements I make in my career, I will always be known as the guy who bit the bat's head off," he told the Associated Press in August, 2000. "Even the Rock and Roll Hall of Fame considers my career a joke because of it."

(Speaking of jokes and jokers, legend has it that Ozzy's dad was none other than Benny Hill. It's not true, but the late, leering comedian and the pie-faced frontman for Black Sabbath *do* have a facial resemblance.)

And then there's Keith Richards of the Rolling Stones—who's still rocking and doesn't look a day over 140—and the legendary stories about him "replenishing" his system by undergoing complete blood transfusions, like some sort of guitarist–vampire in search of fresh blood to keep him going.

The blood transfusion tale is firmly ensconced in rock lore. When *Spin* magazine published its list of "The 100 Sleaziest Moments in Rock" in the August, 2000 issue, No. 65 was Richards getting a total blood transfusion, reportedly to kick his heroin addiction. In Angela Bowie's autobiography, *Backstage Passes: Life on the Wild Side with David Bowie*, she recounted seeing Richards looking "all bright-eyed and peppy after one of those refreshing total blood transfusions." And when Tony Sanchez, a former staffer for the Rolling Stones, wrote a book about his experiences, he claimed Richards had had blood transfusions on several occasions to rid his system of heroin.

In a 1983 interview with *The Washington Post*, Richards confronted the latest rumor—that he'd been born again—and also addressed the blood transfusion stories.

"That's [the born-again rumor] a new one, apart from the blood change, anyway," he said. "Could it be the same thing? I've never had a blood change and I've never been born again, quite honestly. Funny, though, it's the thing people believed about me more than anything else. [But] it's all original blood here. I wouldn't get rid of it. I might wake up and find out I couldn't play anymore."

Besides, getting a blood transfusion isn't as simple as changing the oil in one's car. If that were the case, heroin addicts the world over would be ridding themselves of their demons by getting rid of the old blood for a fresh supply.

It's Not Easy
Being a Green CD

In the beginning of my career as a music buyer, there was the 45, aka "the single," and it was good. The first single I ever bought, at the Ben Franklin store in Riverdale, Ill., was "Bend Me, Shape Me" by American Breed, a plaintive declaration of elastic love ("Bend me, shape me, any way you want me / long as you love me it's all right!") that still is heard and loved in— well, nowhere. Somehow the Eminems and Snoops of the world have yet to sample the unforgettable chorus of this timeless classic. Fools.

Spending my allowance money as fast as I could earn it, I soon filled my case of 45s with three-minute classics by the McCoys, the 1910 Fruitgum Company, Tommy James and the Shondells, and Country Joe and the Fish. (Interesting how those latter two group names work, and yet Tommy James and the

Fish, and Country Joe and the Shondells both sound stupid.) By the time I reached puberty, my tastes had become more refined, more sophisticated—so I joined the Columbia Record Club and started receiving LPs, or "albums," such as *Talking Book* by Stevie Wonder; *Hot August Night* by Neil Diamond; and *Venus and Mars Are All Right Tonight* by Paul McCartney.

Next came tapes known as "8-tracks." The Doobie Brothers. Journey. Ted Nugent. Cheap Trick.

When I went off to college, the 45s were but a memory and the 8-track tapes were long gone, but I still had a thick stack of albums to pack, along with a growing collection of cassettes, known as "cassettes." I sold my albums during my senior year because I needed to eat—but many of those cassettes lasted another decade after college.

And then came the compact disc, aka the CD, which reigns supreme today. Walk into any music store in the country and you'll find row upon row of CDs, and little or no mention of cassettes or vinyl. For vintage stuff like that, you have to visit a specialty store.

Nevertheless, a lot of true audiophiles say that vinyl is vastly superior to the more technically precise but relatively "thin" sound of a CD, which is free of pops and crackles and distortion, but somehow lacks the rich texture of the good old-fashioned record.

There is, however, an inexpensive and ridiculously simple way to enrich the sound of a commercial CD. It's called "greening," and it involves taking a green, felt-tip marker and coloring the outer and inner edges of the disc, making sure you don't touch the actual playing surface of the CD. Wait for the ink to dry, pop the disc into your player, and presto! Instant improvement.

Why would this make a difference? That's not entirely clear, but the theory is that the green coating around the edges of the plastic-and-aluminum disc somehow works against "leakage" from the laser beam that projects onto the disc and creates sound.

And why green? Who knows! One might as well ask why Van Halen specified that only the brown M&Ms be removed from candy dishes backstage!

The venerable J.D. Considine of Baltimore's *The Sun* wrote about the greening phenomenon more than a decade ago, in a piece titled, "The Greening of America, CD Style, Attracts Attention." Considine quoted Dave Herren of the store Audio Alternative in Portland, Ore., who had told a CD newsletter, "[Greening] is really spectacular. I just did it with a Great White CD and was absolutely amazed."

(Okay, I have to say here that there's nothing you can do to a Great White CD that should amaze you. Now on with the quote from Herren.)

"You'd think that the digital recordings would improve the most, but on Phil Collins's *Face Value,* an analog recording, I was flabbergasted—literally astounded."

Considine's piece came on the heels of the 1989 Consumer Electronics Show, where the CD greening story was making the rounds—and the article in the ICE (International CD Exchange) newsletter that he quoted in the story. Some audiophiles even claimed that the best results could be obtained with a specific type of marker—an Eberhard Faber Design Art Marker No. 255—which, incidentally, is more of a turquoise than a green.

In May of 1990, *USA Today* examined the trend:

"'It's amazing that you can improve billion-dollar technology with a two-buck marker,' said Pete Howard of the ICE newsletter.

"'I get a great deal of satisfaction in showing that these tweaks take the "perfect-sound-forever" medium and make it a little more perfect,' added Sam Tellig, a writer for Stereophile."

But a month later, *The New York Times* published a more skeptical piece, with Hans Fantel writing: "Audio fans swallow a lot of nonsense....For example, otherwise sensible people have lately taken to painting their CDs green around the edge in the firm belief that this makes them sound better...[but] this practice is no harmless superstition. It may damage discs and conceivably cause the loss of one's entire CD collection."

The article cited a study by *Inmusic* magazine, which used a digital error counter to compare greened and unmarked discs and found no difference whatsoever. And not only did greening fail to improve sound quality, but the solvents in most markers could eventually eat away at the coating that protects the aluminum layer, thus ruining the disc.

Why is greening useless? Not to get too bogged down in technical jargon, but according to the experts, CDs employ digital technology, which means either the laser can read the numbers and create a uniform musical reproduction, or it can't read the numbers, which would cause the CD to "skip." It's an either/or proposition, thus there's no sliding scale of quality that would allow for an improvement of sound quality.

Years later, however, people were still talking about using a green marker, or Armor All, or even a deep freezer to enhance CDs. Even today you can find Internet and stereo magazine pitches for products like the "CD Stoplight," which retails for about $15 and supposedly improves the sound of CDs by absorbing laser light, and the "CD Tuning Sheet" (usually priced at about $3), a device you attach to the disc to reduce that pesky electrostatic discharge. I haven't tried these products because I like to believe I have a life—but in the interest of research, I bought a standard-issue, green felt-tip marker and conducted an uncontrolled experiment with two copies of David Gray's *White Ladder* CD. I greened one copy and left the other untouched, and asked a friend to place them into a multidisc changer, without telling me which was which, of course. I instructed my friend to play the hit single "Babylon" six straight times, using her discretion. It could be four versions from the greened CD and two from the regular CD; or six in a row from the greened version; whatever. My mission was to try to pick up a difference in sound quality from take to take. It would be sort of the aural version of going to the optometrist and trying to figure out if he's messing with your head when he's showing you rows of letters and saying, "Is this one better—or this one? What about this one? Better still? Or worse?"

This was the order she selected: Greened version of "Babylon." Regular version of "Babylon." Regular. Green. Regular. Regular.

This is what I heard: Same. Same. Same. Same. Same. Same.

Concerned that my cynical attitude might have influenced my reaction, I decided to try the same experiment on another friend, without explaining whether the whole greening theory had any merit to it. I just played the greened and ungreened versions of "Babylon" back to back and asked him if he could notice any difference in sound quality.

He said he thought the ungreened version might have sounded a little bit better.

Evidence notwithstanding, there are still some audiophiles who swear by the greening process. Perhaps the undeniable power of suggestion is enough to truly make a difference for them.

For those true believers, I've got another piece of advice: If you use a red felt-tip marker on your ears, it improves the sound. Don't believe me? Try it!

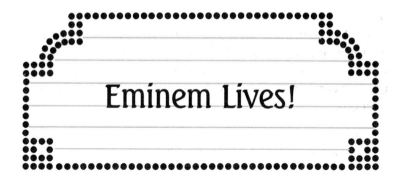

Eminem Lives!

Paul is dead! Elvis is alive! Frank Zappa's dad was Mister Greenjeans! John Denver was a sniper in Vietnam!

You know you've joined the ranks of pop music stardom when you find yourself starring in your very own urban legend. The hits and the adulation and the sold-out stadiums are but wispy, ethereal, passing pleasures—but the urban legend lives on long after the last encore.

The lightning rod of controversy known as Eminem, aka the Real Slim Shady (his birth name is Marshall Mathers III, but that's hardly the kind of moniker that inspires images of a tough guy swaggering across the stage while hollering "Yo! Yo! Yo!" and other deep thoughts), seems to be an urban legend aficionado, if his lyrics are any indication. On the 2000 release "Stan," Eminem raps about the UL that the song "In the Air Tonight" by Phil Collins is the autobiographical story of Collins witnessing a murder by drowning and not doing anything about it—until Collins duped the killer by having him come to a concert as a "contest winner," only to expose the crime by singing about it onstage. (This story is detailed in my book *Urban Legends*.)

Or as Eminem puts it:

You know that song by Phil Collins from "In the Air Tonight"?

About that guy who could have saved that other guy from drowning? But didn't?

Then Phil saw it all then at his show he found him?

On the 1999 single "Cum On Everybody," Eminem raps: "Bought Lauryn Hill's tape so her kids could starve." This is a bit of an illogical non sequitur, but what is clear is that Eminem is talking about the urban legend that has Lauryn Hill saying she would "rather have my children starve than have white people buy my albums."

In late 2000, Eminem starred in an urban legend of his own. After a tumultuous year that included his mother suing him because of his musical claims that she was a dope fiend; a near-divorce with his wife, Kim, highlighted by a barroom brawl with a guy from the Insane Clown Posse who had reportedly been smooching with Kimmie; his grandmother asking him for money so she could pay to have his uncle's body exhumed; the attempted suicide of his estranged wife; protests from women's groups and gay organizations about the lyrical content of his work; and well-crafted feuds with the likes of artists Christina Aguilera, Carson Daly of MTV, *NSync, and Limp Bizkit— after all that—the Real Slim Shady met his fate in a tragic car accident, according to supposed reports by *MTV News* and CNN.com that quickly circulated on the Web in December. There were even pictures of the wreck that supposedly claimed

Eminem's life. (The car in the photo was a sensible Saturn. Now, a Saturn is a fine and sturdy automobile, but come on, does anyone see Eminem in a Saturn? Marshall Mathers, maybe, but not the Real Slim Shady.)

As one reader put it in an e-mail to David Emery, the about.com expert on urban legends:

We read on the Internet on Sunday, December 17 that Slim Shady, aka Eminem, died in a car crash at 2:30 in the morning. According to this article, he was on his way to a late-night party and he was drunk and high on drugs. We can't seem to locate this site. Can you find out if this is true or not?

An anecdote by Neil Strauss in the December 21, 2000, edition of *The New York Times* led with *two* urban legends about Eminem:

"Last weekend a record executive stood at a party displaying news he had just received on his pager. It said Eminem was going to be named *Time* magazine's Man of the Year. The message even included text for the supposed *Time* article. The next day, a report began appearing on music-news Web sites that Eminem had died in a car crash. Both tales, of course, turned out to be false."

Thank God, Eminem was okay. And while we're thanking God, let's give all praise that the editors of *Time* didn't make a pathetic reach for hipster status by selecting Eminem as their Man of the Year. (They went with George W. Bush, aka the Real Shady Past.)

But the Eminem-is-dead rumor picked up so much steam that the rapper's official Web site issued a statement:

Despite sick-minded ne'er do-well attempts to create a state of panic in this grand country by virtue of a well-crafted CNN.com fake news story prank, our beloved Slim Shady is alive and well. Marshall is alive and at home with his family for the holidays in Detroit. And wishes all of you shady holidays and a dirty new year.

Ironic that Eminem's people would say a prank about him dying is "sick-minded," given that the rapper's lyrics have included fantasies about cutting his father's throat and murdering and raping other loved ones.

The *Macomb* (Mich.) *Daily* talked to Eminem's mother, who said, "Someone said he had his head severed in a car accident. I can't believe these rumors keep on persisting."

You'd think Mom would be a bit more savvy about rumors, what with suing her son over allegedly libelous things he's said about her, but there you have it.

As of this writing, Eminem is alive and well. Here's hoping he's healthy and thriving well into his 50s, when we'll no doubt see him on a VH-1 *Behind the Music* special, looking all bald and chubby, weeping while saying, "Eminem was a character who took over my life, but when the fans abandoned me and the record label dropped me, I knew I had to change my ways. And that's when I fell in love with the music of Cole Porter...."

"Fire and Rain"

James Taylor was in his early 20s when he penned "Fire and Rain," one of the most powerful and moving ballads ever recorded about the pain of loss. With the instantly familiar acoustic guitar opening that soon meets up with the somber piano chords, you can feel the ache of longing even before Taylor begins to sing in a sweet, sad voice: "Just yesterday morning, they let me know you were gone, Suzanne the plans they made put an end to you...."

Of all the singer-songwriters of the 1960s and 1970s, none was more sensitive and poetic than the young James Taylor. Even his demons were spectacularly romantic and darkly attractive: his suicidal rages as a teenager; the bout with mental illness that necessitated a nine-month stay in a mental institution; his addiction to heroin; his tumultuous marriage to Carly Simon.

And then there was the famous Suzanne of "Fire and Rain." When Taylor sings about "the plans they made," he's talking about her funeral arrangements, yes? And the chorus, with its tagline of, "But I always thought that I'd see you again," tells us that James didn't see it coming. He had no idea his beloved Suzanne was in such pain.

Or, wait. Maybe she wasn't a suicide at all! Maybe she was the casualty of a plane crash. Consider this posting, which appears on a fascinating Web site called "Meanings of Lyrics of Songs from the 1970s":

Someone put on this page that ["Fire and Rain"] was about a woman who was with him in the mental ward. Although he was in a mental ward (1970's answer to heroin rehab) and he did write a song about that ("Knockin Round the Zoo"), this song is not about that. Here is the real story: When James Taylor went off to record his first album shortly after he was signed, his girlfriend, Susan, had to stay at home. They could not afford a ticket for her, and since it was 1970 and he was a new artist, the label did not front the money. As a surprise, as he was finishing up on the album, his friends and the label pitched in to fly Susan to be with him. Tragically, the airplane crashed and she was killed. Since it was a surprise, he did not hear about it until after he finished the album and the label told him what had happened. Isn't that sad?

Hmmm, so that's what Taylor meant when he sang about "Sweet dreams and flying machines in pieces on the ground." But even if his girlfriend's visit was to be a "surprise," was Taylor so sequestered that he had no contact with the outside world, whether it would be news organizations reporting on the crash or loved ones who would want to tell him what happened? And who were these people who didn't tell Taylor about the plane crash until after he had finished the album? If that had really happened, wouldn't he have recorded a song titled, "I'd Like to Throttle the Heartless Bastards at My Record Company for Not Telling Me My Girlfriend Was Killed"?

Fan postings on a James Taylor Web site tell these versions of the story:

Something I heard about this line goes like this: JT had a girlfriend that he was really focusing on. Some friends decided that she was a bad influence on him, and convinced her to go away for a while. They bought her a plane ticket, she got on the plane, and en route, it crashed and she was killed in the accident. She was the "sweet dream," and the plane was the "flying machine."

The real story behind "Fire and Rain," as I understand it, is that some friends of James's were going to surprise James by bringing his girlfriend, Suzanne, to one of his concerts, unbeknownst to James. According to the story, Suzanne's plane crashed ("sweet dreams and flying machines in pieces on the ground") on her way to see the concert and Suzanne dies ("Suzanne the plans they made put an end to you").

"Fire and Rain" was written about a friend of JT's, Suzanne. They met when they were in Austin Riggs for heroin addiction. They became very close "friends." After JT was released, they spoke on the phone a lot, helping each other out ("hours of time on the telephone line"). Suzanne was supposed to be released, but committed suicide very close to her release date. The line "Sweet dreams and flying machines in pieces on the ground" refers to JT's past— and the breakup of his first band (Flying Machine).

So which is it—suicidal girlfriend, or girlfriend killed in a plane crash?

Neither. Parts of "Fire and Rain" are about suicide, but Suzanne wasn't really Taylor's girlfriend—she was a friend of his. Taylor himself was so fragile at the time that friends didn't think he could handle the news, so he wasn't told of Suzanne's death until a few months after the fact. (Not to disparage for a moment the feelings Taylor had for this troubled young woman—but if they'd been extremely close, that is, boyfriend and girlfriend, wouldn't he have been trying to get in touch with her during the interim? How could her suicide have been shielded from him for months?) The first verse—and probably the chorus—is about Suzanne. But that's just one element of a mini-trilogy of events covered in the song. Verse two deals with Taylor's drug addiction: "Won't you look down upon me Jesus, you gotta help me make a stand/You just got to see me through another day...."

And at least part of the third verse seems to be about the breakup of a band Taylor was in, called The Flying Machine: "Sweet dreams and flying machines in pieces on the ground." In the February 18, 1971, edition of *Rolling Stone* magazine, Taylor said, "The first verse was a reaction to a friend of mine killing herself....The second verse of it is about my kicking junk just before I left England. And the third verse is about my going into a hospital in Western Massachusetts. It's just a hard-time song, a blues without having the blues form."

In *Fire and Rain: The James Taylor Story*, the controversial author (Ian Halperin) repeats many of the ULs mentioned here, but also makes the claim that Taylor has "privately...admitted" to friends that Suzanne was a girl he met while in the Austin Riggs mental hospital. Several months after Taylor left the institution, he learned that Suzanne had killed herself. (Halperin also reports that "Fire and Rain" was in constant rotation on Elvis Presley's turntable in the weeks before the King died.)

Dozens of concert reviews and newspaper articles about Taylor use the shorthand of saying "Fire and Rain" is about "a friend's suicide." The more complex and layered meaning of Taylor's signature classic doesn't dilute its power an iota, but it does mean that the commonly believed interpretation of "Fire and Rain" is more urban legend than pop music fact.

"The Little Girl"

In late summer of 2000, Nashville songwriter Harley Allen and country singer John Michael Montgomery teamed up to do something that has rarely been done before, even though it seems like an obvious idea.

They turned an urban legend into a hit song.

Think about all the great little self-contained stories that exist in the UL canon, from the vanishing hitchhiker to the killer with a hook on his hand to the story of the bride who cancels the wedding after announcing that her groom-to-be had slept with her maid of honor. Goofy urban legends could be turned into novelty songs, while myths about infidelity are perfect fodder for country-western singers and religious ULs for Christian artists. Heavy metal players could have fun with satanic-themed and/or serial killer ULs, and rappers could use fables about love and murder and gang initiations as material.

Hey, it's not like you're going to get sued for stealing somebody else's story. For that to happen, someone would have to step forward and prove that he or she is the original creator of an urban legend, and we all know that such a thing never happens, because these stories are almost always impossible to trace back to square one.

Urban legends have been implemented in dozens of movies, books, and TV shows, but I can't recall a single pop hit that is a direct interpretation of a familiar UL—that is, until the aforementioned Mr. Allen wrote a song entirely based on an Internet e-mail that's been circulating for at least a half-dozen years. It's usually titled "And the Little Child Shall Lead Them" or "Held by Jesus," and it's been used in church sermons and appears on a number of Christian Web sites as well.

Here's one version:

There was an atheist couple who were nothing but trouble. He was a drinker and she was a drug addict, and neither one of them could hold down a job. To make matters worse, they were atheists. When they had a little baby girl, they never once told her a single thing about our Lord.

One night when the girl was five years old, her parents got into a terrible fight that ended with the dad shooting the mom and killing her, and then turning the gun on himself and committing suicide. The frightened little girl witnessed all of this.

The authorities came, and the little girl was sent to a foster home where she was welcomed by loving parents who believed in God. On the first day of Sunday School, the foster mother took the teacher aside and said, "She's never been taught anything about Jesus, so please be patient with her." The teacher said, "I understand."

The teacher began class by holding up a picture of Jesus and saying, "Does anyone know who this is?"

To the teacher's surprise, the little girl raised her hand and said, "I do. That's the man who was holding me the night my parents died."

Sure, it's sentimental and manipulative—and if you're a nonbeliever or if your faith takes you in a different direction, you might be rolling your eyes at the pure schmaltz of it all. But as parables go, it's powerful and effective on a basic level.

Still, there's nothing in that well-circulated e-mail to indicate that the story is anything but a nicely crafted little story to make a point in Christian teachings.

According to press reports, Harley Allen, who has written hits for Linda Ronstadt, Garth Brooks, Alan Jackson, and many others, came across the story in the late 1990s.

"My brother sent it to me in an e-mail," he told Nashville's *The Tennessean*. "I tried to trace it to where it came from, but I never could find out whether it was true or a legend."

Allen told *USA Today*, "[The e-mail] moved me more than I'd been moved in years by a story. I grabbed the guitar and just started writing. It didn't take any time at all, about 10 or 15 minutes."

The result was "The Little Girl," a more detailed version of the fable. It begins:

Her parents never took the young girl to church
Never spoke of His name
Never read her His word...

Allen's lyrics go on to talk about the "drinking and the fighting," and how things went from bad to worse, "until her daddy in a drunk rage one night, used a gun on her mom and then took his life." The little girl is taken in by a "new mom and dad," and on the "first day of Sunday School," she sees

Jesus on the cross and says she knows "that man," as he was the one who held her close the night her parents died.

Montgomery laid down a traditional, clean, acoustic and steel guitar-driven track and contributed an understated but strong vocal (backed by Alison Krauss and Dan Tyminski) that further distinguished "The Little Girl" from the typically slick fare playing on country stations these days. Even before Montgomery's *Brand New Me* album was officially released, "The Little Girl" was leaked to radio stations and became an immediate sensation—the kind of tune that prompts an inordinate number of calls from listeners asking about the title and artist.

"It's the biggest reaction record we've had all year," Jon Anthony of WMZQ in Washington, D.C., told Montgomery's Web site, which also quoted Travis Moon of KEEY-FM saying, "We played the song once and got about 75 calls. This song ranks in the Top 5 of all time in positive testing in the history of the station.…" At the end of 2000, "The Little Girl" was listed as the 10th biggest hit of the year in country music.

And in a bizarre, real-life development that sounds like an urban legend or at least like something you'd see on *The Practice* or *Ally McBeal*, a judge in Washington, Pa., actually played the song at the conclusion of a murder trial. In November of 2000, Michelle Sue Tharp was convicted of first-degree murder in the 1998 starvation death of her 7-year-old daughter, Tausha Lee Lanham. The poor child had been born three months premature and weighed just 12 pounds at the time of her death. After the jury took three hours to find Tharp guilty and only one hour to find in favor of the death penalty, Washington County (Pa.) Judge Paul Pozonsky delayed the official announcement and set up a boom box in the courtroom with the *Brand New Me* CD cued to "The Little Girl." The song was played without comment by Judge Pozonsky before he read the jury's decision. As of this writing, Tharp's attorneys are asking for a new trial, in part because of what they believe was biased and inappropriate behavior by the judge, including the playing of "The Little Girl" in court.

Blondie
Blunts Bundy?

Whenever a notorious serial killer is brought to justice, any individual who once crossed his path but for some reason was spared, is probably overwhelmed by a palette of emotions that includes relief, gratitude, guilt—and a serious case of the chills. Try to imagine the whirlwind of feelings: You'd thank fate for sparing you, you'd feel bad for those who weren't so fortunate—and you'd experience a retroactive wave of terror washing over you as you realized that you, too, could have been a victim.

As a reporter in Chicago, I've talked to a couple of guys who, as teenagers, worked for or had a passing acquaintance with the notorious "Killer Clown," John Wayne Gacy; more than two decades later, they're still freaked out by the thoughts of "what if."

And so it is with singer Deborah Harry, and her chillingly close call with none other than Ted Bundy. It's a night she'll never forget.

Harry is the singer and actress best known for her lead vocals with the group Blondie on such late 1970s and early 1980s classics as "Heart of Glass," "Call Me," and "The Tide Is High." Bundy was the notoriously charming and handsome monster who was executed for the murders of three Florida college students. He was held responsible for dozens of other killings in a reign of terror that spanned two arrests and two escapes from prison—and saw him roam through the states of Washington, Idaho, Oregon, Colorado, Utah, and Florida in search of victims.

On January 24, 1989, after years of trials and appeals and stays of execution, Ted Bundy was put to death in the electric chair in Florida. A few months after that, Harry gave an interview to Nestor Aparicio, whose story subsequently appeared in the *St. Petersburg Times*, the *St. Louis Post-Dispatch,* and the *Baltimore Evening Sun*.

"The way Deborah Harry recounts the story is absolutely frightening," Aparicio's story begins. "The rock singer, best known for her work in the post-disco, new-wave band Blondie, was just trying to hail a cab.

"It nearly ended in disaster."

Aparicio then quotes Harry's harrowing tale of trying to flag down a cab on the lower east side of Greenwich Village in New York late one night in the early 1970s:

"A little white car pulls up, and the guy offers me a ride...he was very persistent, and he asked where I was going....I got in the car, and it was summertime and the windows were all rolled up except about an inch and a half at the top. So I was sitting there and he wasn't really talking to me. Automatically, I sort of reached to roll down the window and I realized there was no door handle, no window crank, nothing. The inside of the car was totally stripped out.

"I got very nervous. I reached my arm out through the little crack and stretched down and opened the car from the outside. As soon as he saw that, he tried to turn the corner really fast, and I spun out of the car and landed in the middle of the street."

Harry goes on to explain that after Bundy was executed, she read about him and realized that he'd been the man in the car.

"I hadn't thought about that incident in years. The whole description of how he operated and what he looked like and the kind of car he drove and the time frame he was doing that in that area of the country fit exactly. I said, 'My God, it was him.'

"I'm one of the lucky ones."

Well now. First of all, it's hard to believe that anyone, even a rock star living in the fast lane, only became aware of Bundy and his infamously evil deeds after Bundy's execution. How did Harry miss the years of front-page headlines and TV reports and magazine articles and books about Bundy that had flooded the nation's consciousness for a decade-plus prior to his execution?

More damaging to Harry's credibility is that there are many exhaustively researched and documented accounts of Bundy's travels, from his first murderous exploits in the late 1960s through his haphazard travels in the 1970s to his final arrest in 1978—and none of these accounts ever place Bundy anywhere near New York City.

Harry claims the incident occurred in the early 1970s. Bundy was in the state of Washington for most of that period, working for the King County Law and Justice Planning Office and then attending law school at the University of Puget Sound in Tacoma. He also worked at the Emergency Services Department in Olympia, Wash., before leaving the state in August of 1974 to attend the University of Utah Law School. He also spent time in Idaho, Colorado, and Oregon in the early or mid-1970s, but no reliable source places him within a hundred miles of New York City during those years. And Bundy's car at the time was an ordinary Volkswagen, not a car with the inside stripped out, as Harry put it in the newspaper interview.

Deborah Harry may well have had a frightening encounter in the early 1970s with a man who resembled Ted Bundy—but the evidence is overwhelming that the man in question was *not* the infamous serial killer.

Puffy Dragon

Ben Stiller's Greg Focker is riding in the car with his future father-in-law (played by Robert DeNiro) in an early scene from *Meet the Parents* that's designed to show us that DeNiro's character is a hopeless square who will soon have deep suspicions about Greg's interest in recreational drugs. Peter, Paul & Mary's whimsical hit "Puff the Magic Dragon" comes on the radio, and Stiller tries to make conversation by referencing the "real meaning" of the song—it's about the joys of marijuana.

DeNiro is completely baffled. He's never heard this explanation before and he can't imagine that anyone other than a druggie would know about such things. He squints at Stiller and says, "Are you a pothead, Focker?"

That the makers of a hit comedy in the year 2000 would assume that most of the audience would understand the inside reference to a 35-year-old pop hit is an endorsement of the "Puff the Magic Dragon" legacy. Ironically, though, it's Stiller's character who doesn't understand the true meaning of the song—for "Puff the Magic Dragon" is actually about...a magic dragon.

In an era where crotch-grabbing, pierced, and tattooed pop stars sing freely about pot, speed, coke, heroin, murder, infidelity, robbery, prison life, gangbanging, and rape, the music revolution of the 1960s seems almost cute and quaint by comparison. A bunch of long-haired hippies in fringe jackets singing about the pleasures of spending the night with someone or the joys of altering one's consciousness? Ooohhhh, rebels!

But that's what the mainstream culture was like in the 1960s. The Rolling Stones had to change "Let's Spend the Night Together" to "Let's Spend Some Time Together" when they appeared on *The Ed Sullivan Show*, and The Doors were banned from that same program after Jim Morrison defied an edict not to sing "You know we couldn't get much *higher*" when the band played "Light My Fire." And of course the muddy lyrics to the Kingsmen's "Louie, Louie" were the source of great controversy.

Drug references were often implied or buried within seemingly innocuous or carefully coded lyrics. What were The Byrds singing about in "Eight Miles High"? Was "Lucy in the Sky With Diamonds" a tribute to LSD? (John Lennon always maintained that the title came from a drawing done by his son Julian of a schoolmate named Lucy.) What was putting Jimi Hendrix in that "Purple Haze"? Just who was this "Candy Man" that Sammy Davis Jr. was touting, anyway? And when Steppenwolf sang about a "Magic Carpet Ride," exactly what kind of a trip were they proposing? Hmmmmm.

Then again, it didn't take a genius to ascertain that Jefferson Airplane's "White Rabbit" ("One pill makes you larger, one pill makes you small") was about drug use. And many other hits from the 1960s were fairly obvious in their meaning, for example, Marianne Faithful's "Sister Morphine," Manfred Mann's "LSD," the Small Faces' "Itchycoo Park" ("What will we do there? We'll get high!"), and Lou Reed's "Heroin," to name just a handful.

So why was there such a fracas over "Puff the Magic Dragon," and why is there still debate about the true origins of the song nearly four decades later?

Two factors: First, the song was released in 1962 and peaked on the charts in early 1963, putting it just ahead of the get-high curve. If "Puff" had come out just two or three years later, its supposedly winking lyrics about a boy named Jackie Paper and a dragon ("drag on") named Puff would hardly have been noticed amidst the cacophony of drug-related songs on the charts.

Second, "Puff the Magic Dragon" was marketed as a children's song, rendered by three nice, friendly Bohemian types who didn't seem all that different from the nice young people who were singing at Catholic "guitar masses" or teaching second grade in the 1960s. You know, the kind of people who were against the war but still respected their elders and weren't too cool to admit they dug the music of the Singing Nun. That Peter, Paul & Mary would be trying to poison young minds with an insidious fairy tale that was really an endorsement of marijuana was nothing short of scandalous!

By way of background: In the late 1950s, a college student named Leonard Lipton, who had read and enjoyed an Ogden Nash poem called "Really-O Truly O-Dragon," decided to write his own dragon-centric ditty about a child growing up and leaving behind the imaginary world he had created. Lipton showed the poem to his friend Peter Yarrow, who added some lyrics of his own and put the compilation to music, calling it "Puff the Magic Dragon." A few years later, the folk trio known as Peter, Paul & Mary turned "Puff" into a major hit.

Puff the magic dragon, lived by the sea
And frolicked in the autumn mist in a land called
Honalee....

After the song hit the charts and became a concert favorite, rumors started circulating that the words "puff" and "dragon" were marijuana references; that "Jackie Paper" was an allusion to rolling papers; that the "sea" Puff lived near was a *c* for cocaine; that the "autumn mist" was a cloud of marijuana smoke; and that Honalee was supposedly a secret but very real locale where drug abusers recovered from their addiction.

I think people were smoking a lot of pot when they came up with some of these "signals." These were the same folks who later asserted that TV shows like *H.R. Pufnstuf* and *The Banana Splits* were obvious tributes to the drug culture. Hey, smoke enough reefer or drop enough acid and you can find drug references anywhere.

Lipton always maintained his original intent was to write a bittersweet little tale about a child entering the adult world without looking back. Yarrow has been debunking the dope connotations to the song for more than 30 years; to prove his point, he has sometimes done a concert routine in which he "proves" that any song, even "The Star-Spangled Banner," can be interpreted as an endorsement of drugs.

Yarrow and his fellow bandmates have also refuted the rumor in countless interviews and stage performances.

"As the principal writer of the song, I can assure you, it's a song about innocence lost," he told the *Houston Chronicle* in 1995. "It's easier to interpret 'The Star-Spangled Banner' as a drug song than 'Puff the Magic Dragon.' This is just a funny rumor that was promulgated by *Newsweek* magazine. There is no basis for it. It's inane at this point and really unfortunate, because even in Hong Kong, it's not played because of the allegations [that] it's about drugs. But I assure you, it's not."

In a 1984 letter to *The New York Times*, Yarrow wrote: "Let's get it straight once and for all. 'Puff the Magic Dragon' is not about drugs. It is inane to assert that 'Puff' is about anything other than the sadness of lost childhood innocence."

"It's just a children's song!" Mary Travers said during an October 21, 2000, concert at the Kravis Center in Palm Beach, Fla.

Cynics might say Yarrow and Co. doth protest too much—but for what reason? If "Puff the Magic Dragon" really was about marijuana use, why wouldn't the writers and/or performers acknowledge it? What, they're going to get thrown in retroactive songwriters' jail for advocating pot use in the early 1960s?

Believe what you want. I choose to believe the people who created the song. If they say "Puff" should be taken literally, the interpretation of the tune as a story about pot is nothing more than an urban legend.

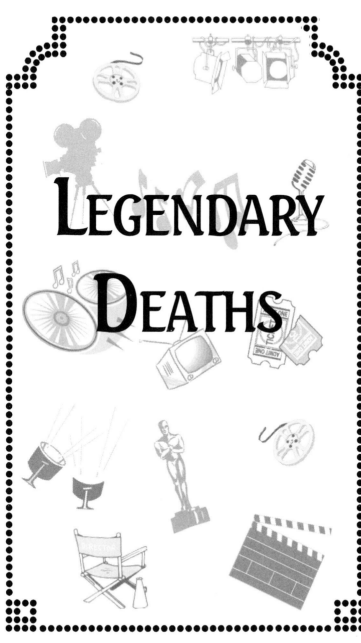

LEGENDARY

DEATHS

Mama Cass and the Ham Sandwich

Poor Cass Elliot. Born Ellen Naomi Cohen, she was an intelligent, interesting, wisecracking hippie Earth Mother with a ribald sense of humor, a hearty appetite for food and men, and a pure, clear voice that was a key ingredient in the beautiful vocal blending of The Mamas and The Papas on such classic hits as "Dedicated to the One I Love," "Monday, Monday," "I Saw Her Again," and "California Dreamin'." With her sweeping bell-bottomed jeans, colorful tunics, and glimmering costume jewelry, her straight hair falling in her face and her oversized profile, Cass was a unique figure on the pop scene in the 1960s.

But in death, Mama Cass has been reduced to an easy reference that everybody gets—a one-liner that has been mentioned in countless newspaper articles, has been the basis for jokey parade floats and avant-garde art, and was even referenced in the first *Austin Powers* movie.

You know how the one-liner goes: Mama Cass choked to death on a ham sandwich.

Probably no other "fact" about Cass is so widely known. People who were born after she died, non-fans who couldn't identify a Mamas and Papas song on a bet—just say the name "Mama Cass" to them and they'll reply with depressing predictability that she choked on a ham sandwich.

"Mama Cass Elliot, the zaftig pop diva, reportedly choked to death on a ham sandwich," claimed an article titled "Death Can Be the End of a Good Reputation" in the *Fort Worth Star Telegram* in 1999. The writer went on to say, "Tasteless jokes are still told about her."

True, and it's mostly due to the continued dissemination of the ham sandwich story.

"Mama Cass choked on a ham sandwich in 1974," asserted the *Chicago Tribune* in a 1990 article.

After the asphyxiation death of INXS lead singer Michael Hutchence in 1997, the *Scottish Daily Record* published a long story about Hutchence and other rock stars who had died before their time, from Marvin Gaye to John Lennon to Kurt Cobain:

"Roly-poly Mama Cass Elliot was the strangest case of all," wrote Melanie Reid. "She was 33 when she was found dead in bed in 1974 with a half-eaten ham sandwich in her hand."

The most famous ham sandwich in modern history was also once featured in a Mardi Gras parade, and it was part of a 1978 exhibit in Washington billed as the "First Annual Edible Art Event." The collection included such folklore-inspired works as "Suburban Trick or Treat" (an apple with a razor blade sticking out) and the "Mama Cass Memorial Ham," a ham sandwich with a bite taken out of it, encased in a plastic baggie.

Rock stars of the world, be careful how you live, and especially how you exit, this mortal coil. Your last few moments could become a more enduring part of your legacy than any song you sang, any person you loved, any child you parented.

So what killed Mama Cass? It wasn't a single sandwich. More accurately, it was the thousands and thousands of sandwiches she consumed before that last one.

Decades before Oprah and Roseanne experienced yo-yo weight gains and losses, Cass struggled mightily with her life-long obesity. Her all-time high was a reported 294 pounds, which would be a dangerous amount of poundage for a 6′ man, let alone a 5′5″ woman. In the late 1960s and early 1970s, the desperate Cass often resorted to fad crash diets, including one program that had her fasting four days a week. After seven months of this insane ritual, Cass had lost more than 100 pounds—but she had to be hospitalized, and she never was the same after that. Her health was a constant issue in the years to come.

In 1974, Cass was trying another extremely dangerous diet—this one had her eating just one full meal a week—but she felt strong enough to fly to London for two weeks worth of sold-out engagements at the famed Palladium. Cass stayed in the Mayfair apartment of Harry Nilsson, the singer/songwriter behind "Without You" and "Everybody's Talkin'," the theme from *Midnight Cowboy*. (In fact, it was the same apartment in which Keith Moon had died in 1974 after one too many nights of excessive imbibing.) Elliot managed to make it through those two weeks of shows, but two nights after the final gig, her body was found in bed in the apartment, a sandwich reportedly on the table by her side. She was 32. (Some accounts list Cass as 33, but she was six weeks shy of her 33rd birthday when she died.)

A physician who noted the sandwich by Elliot's side told the press that she had "probably choked on a sandwich." Within a day, some accounts in the American press had it as a "ham sandwich," though at least one former bandmate finds fault with that detail.

"What is a Jewish girl eating ham for anyway?" said Denny Doherty in a January 30, 2000, piece in *The New York Times*. "It didn't happen. Her poor old heart just quit."

Doherty has forensic pathology on his side. Dr. Keith Simpson performed the autopsy on Elliot, and Dr. Gavin Thurston was the coroner on duty at the time. They both concluded that Elliot had died from a heart attack that was brought on by her obesity. (Her weight at the time of death was 238 pounds.) The physicians found no evidence of food or vomit blocking the trachea and concluded that she hadn't eaten much of anything the several hours before her death.

These facts were reported by the press, but by then, the ham sandwich stories were flying about and couldn't be tamed. Other rumors also began to circulate: that Cass had died of a heroin overdose; that Cass had been carrying John Lennon's baby at the time of her death. These, too, are pure fiction.

By the time she was 32, Mama Cass might have done too much damage to her heart to have survived even if she had lost weight in a healthy, gradual manner under a doctor's supervision. The ultimate irony, though, is that her lack of eating in the summer of 1974 was deemed a factor in her demise.

But it's easy to make those cracks about the fat lady choking down one last ham sandwich—which then chokes her.

In that same *New York Times* article that quotes Doherty, Elliot's daughter Owen, who was 7 when her mother died, says, "It's been hard for my family with the sandwich rumor. One last slap against the fat lady. People seem to think it's funny. What's so darn funny?"

Owen elaborated on her thoughts in an interview for this book:

Q. "What do you think of the reporters who continue to print false rumors about your mother's death?"

A. "I think that the reporters who continue to falsely report the cause of my mother's death are only uneducated. One would think that before doing a story, a journalist would fact-check! My mother's autopsy report stated that my mother died of heart failure. I think that the media 'ate up' the story about the ham sandwich. I also believe it was amusing, to some sickos, that a woman who so obviously struggled with her weight had apparently died from eating.

"There was a sandwich found by her bed, half eaten. This is where the story started. It was perpetuated forever. Believe me, this is a very sensitive subject, one that is extremely painful for my family."

Q. "Would you say that it's true that your mother's dieting weakened her heart, which led to her death?"

A. "It played a part, I'm sure. But there is a history of heart problems in my family."

Q. "How would you prefer your mother to be remembered?"

A. "I would like my mother to be remembered for who she was: a trusted and loyal friend. Someone who loved unconditionally. Someone who is remembered for her accomplishments."

If there's to be a one-line epitaph for Mama Cass Elliot, it should not be about a ham sandwich. It should be simply this: She had a beautiful voice, more timeless than any urban legend.

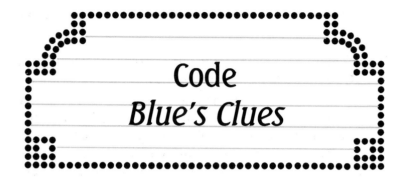

Code
Blue's Clues

In the 21st century, the dead-celebrity rumor often seems to be the work of Internet pranksters. They're not innocently passing along a story they heard and believe to be true; they're deliberately and carefully constructing a fabrication—often making it look like a news bulletin on an Internet version of a respected news organization, such as the Associated Press or CNN—and letting it loose on the World Wide Web, knowing full well it will be picked up and repeated ad infinitum.

Around Thanksgiving of 1998, the likely scenario is that somebody sitting in front of a computer somewhere decided it would be fun to "kill off" Steve Burns, the rugby shirt-wearing, preternaturally cheerful host of the popular *Blue's Clues* children's show on the Nickelodeon network.

If you haven't seen the show: *Blue's Clues* pairs Burns with an animated blue dog. He asks the preschoolers watching at home to look for clues—blue paw prints—as they appear on the screen. When such clues appear, Burns writes them down, and with the help of such animated characters as Mr. Salt and Mrs. Pepper, as well as kids watching at home, he solves the riddle of the day.

Millions of little kids love *Blue's Clues* and its host—so for someone to start or deliberately spread the rumor that Steve Burns had died is a particularly insidious thing to do, because you know that it wouldn't just be cafeteria conversation among adults, it would be a story that would trickle down to very young children.

The story making the rounds was that Burns had been killed in a car crash. After a few weeks, when it was obvious that Burns was very much alive, as he was still showing up on *Blue's Clues*, the rumor was that he had been replaced by a look-alike, a la The Beatles supposedly finding a stand-in for Paul McCartney in the late 1960s.

One possible source of inspiration for the *Blue's Clues* rumor: In 1995, the same year he began his run on the Nickelodeon show, Burns (then billed as "Steven Burns") did a guest shot on *Law and Order* in which he played an autistic youth who died while in police custody. Did someone catch a rerun of that episode three years later and somehow confuse television and reality? Perhaps a young *Blue's Clues* fan was watching the show with a taunting older sibling who convinced the kid that Steve was really dead.

Burns' own mother called him at one point, just to make sure he was okay.

In a 1999 *New York Times* story about the rumor, *Blue's Clues* chief writer and co-creator Angela Santomero said, "[This] is very different from [the] Paul McCartney [rumors]. It's very different when these are 2- to 5-year-old children you're talking about. Steve has become someone they trust, someone they almost have a play date with and go on adventures with, and thinking he might not be there anymore is really upsetting to them."

Which was probably the sick intention of whomever created the rumor in the first place. And a second wave of rumors was even nastier—now the story was that Burns had become hooked on heroin and had died of an overdose.

Burns confronted the rumors head-on.

"Steve isn't laughing," his publicist told *USA Today*. "He's worried that people were going to start saying he was doing drugs. He was really creeped out about it. He's very sensitive."

In December, 1998, Burns accepted Rosie O'Donnell's invitation to come on her show and have an exchange specifically targeted to little kids.

"How are you?" asked Rosie.

"I feel great!" replied Burns.

Burns and Santomero also appeared on the *Today Show* and talked about the best ways for parents to discuss the rumor with their children. (One suggestion I might have made: "Have the kids watch us right now!") He also continued taping episodes of *Blue's Clues* in New York, made several appearances at various forums on children's television, and did interviews with newspaper reporters.

"He walked in the door, and the rumor flew out the window," wrote John Kiesewetter in the *Cincinnati Enquirer* in September of 1999. "Steve Burns, host of Nickelodeon's hugely popular *Blue's Clues*, was not dead. Indeed he was standing right there in front of several reporters. According to rumors on the Internet, Steve Burns had been killed in a car wreck or overdosed on drugs. Where did the rumors come from?"

"We have no idea," said Burns.

In early 2001, Burns announced he would be stepping down as host of *Blue's Clues*. It's almost a given that when Burns does leave, it will revive the stories about him getting killed. *He's not on the show because he's not on the face of the Earth!*

Sigh.

INTERESTING NOTE: About a year before the Burns rumors started circulating, Scott Baio was the victim of a similar wave of stories, fueled by several radio reports that he had been killed in a car crash. Baio's own parents reportedly were sobbing hysterically when they called his home to find out if the reports were true.

"After a while I started answering the phone: 'I'm not dead,'" Baio told *The New York Times Magazine*.

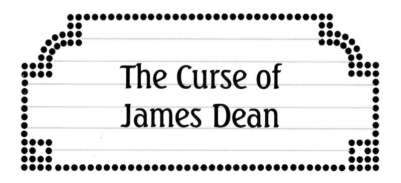

The Curse of
James Dean

Death was a great career move for James Dean.

When he crashed his new Porsche Spyder 550 convertible on September 30, 1955, the 24-year-old Dean had done just three movies—and the only one that had been released, *East of Eden*, was a moderate hit. Dean's other two films, *Rebel Without a Cause* and *Giant*, came out after his death, and by then the cult of James Dean was already overtaking the more complex and darker truths about the real Dean.

Who knows where Dean's career would have taken him had he lived to a ripe old age? There's no disputing his talent, but he was an unpopular character with producers, directors, many of his fellow actors, and even the security guards who were frustrated by his reckless driving on studio lots. At 24, Dean had already carved out a reputation in the business as an egomaniacal, sexually adventurous, sometimes cruel and cynical operator.

"I hated his guts," said Rock Hudson. "And he probably hated mine."

"He was the glorification of hatred," said Elia Kazan.

"Dean suffered from success poisoning, despite all that his image stood for," said novelist Edna Ferber, who wrote *Giant*.

James Dean would have turned 70 on February 8, 2001. Perhaps he would have mellowed and matured into a responsible, dependable actor, with a roller-coaster career of ups and downs—everything from Academy Award-nominated roles in critically acclaimed blockbusters to a TV series in the 1970s playing a wisecracking private detective. Or maybe he would have found another way to burn out.

By dying, Dean became an idol. Sales of memorabilia bearing his name and likeness total more than $80 million a year (he's particularly popular in Japan), and his legend has spawned a number of movies, songs, and works of fiction.

Dean's hometown of Fairmount, Ind., has become a Mecca for young fans who come from all over the world to visit the landmarks of his youth and the cemetery where he was laid to rest. (Dean was actually born in nearby Marion, Ind., but his family moved to Fairmount when he was a baby.) I visited Fairmount a few years ago and toured the attractions, starting with the James Dean Memorial Gallery, a seven-room Victorian house filled with photographs, letters, clothes, paintings, posters, grade-school artwork and writing assignments, and even a likeness of Dean from the Coney Island Wax Museum. In a small room near the back of the house, a monitor shows a continuous, 30-minute loop of movie scenes, commercials, outtakes, and television appearances from Dean's brief career. "You're not listening to me!" Dean screams at his father (played by Jim Backus, aka Mr. Howell on *Gilligan's*

Island) in a scene from *Rebel Without a Cause*. (Imagine working the counter in this place and hearing that scene twice an hour, eight hours a day, five days a week.)

After stopping at Dean's old high school and the Fairmount Museum (which also has an exhibit of Dean memorabilia), I made the pilgrimage to Park Cemetery and the unspectacular pink granite tombstone with the simple inscription: "James B. Dean, 1931–1955." Ruby lipstick imprints were kissed onto the stone. Someone had left a small photograph of Dean's sister legend, Marilyn Monroe. A note half-buried in a flowerpot read: "I came here from Belgium. I am 21 years old. Too fast to live, too young to die, bye-bye."

The headstone has been stolen twice, recovered twice. And it's been damaged so much by overzealous fans—some chipping away pieces to take home as macabre souvenirs—that it had to be replaced by a new stone.

Such is the glamour and the weirdness attached to the legend of James Dean.

Dean's death has also spawned talk of chilling, unexplained phenomena:

★ The car itself is said to be haunted. Automobile designer George Barris bought the Porsche Spyder from Dean's estate. When the car was delivered to his storage facility in Los Angeles, it came loose from the truck and slammed into a mechanic, breaking his legs.

★ Barris sold the engine of the Porsche to Troy McHenry, a Beverly Hills doctor. McHenry had the engine put into a Porsche—and was killed the first time he drove it.

- ★ The transmission, Barris claimed, was sold to a man who was later in a car wreck and who was left partially paralyzed.

- ★ Even the ultimate fate of the Spyder's shell is in dispute. One story says that a truck carrying the shell of the car was in an accident, and the shell was stolen from the roadside. But Barris said he put the shell on display in a traveling exhibit, and he last saw the Spyder in 1958 at a car show in Florida, after which it was presumably stolen.

  Perhaps its final resting place is in a junkyard next to the car from *Christine*.

Many of Dean's peers and associates have died prematurely and in dramatic fashion—sparking talk of a "James Dean curse":

- ★ Sal Mineo, Dean's co-star in *Rebel Without a Cause*, was stabbed to death in a fight with a male lover in Los Angeles in 1976.

- ★ Dean's love interest in the movie, Natalie Wood, was on a yacht with her husband, Robert Wagner, and actor Christopher Walken in 1981, when she mysteriously drowned in the middle of the night.

- ★ Dean's *Giant* co-star Rock Hudson died of AIDS.

- ★ *Rebel Without a Cause* director, Nicholas Ray, lost an eye in a barroom brawl, became a cocaine addict, and died of cancer in 1979.

- ★ The film's producer, David Weisbert, died at the age of 45 in 1967.

- ★ Dean's friend Nick Adams died of a drug overdose in 1968.

★ Pier Angeli, an actress who had an affair with Dean but left him for Vic Damone, drugged herself to death in 1971, leaving behind a note saying, "Love is far behind me; it was killed at the wheel of a Porsche."

★ Other co-stars and friends of Dean's, including Elizabeth Taylor and Dennis Hopper, have barely survived addictions and illnesses.

Then again, there are hundreds of people who knew and worked with Dean who weren't felled by tragedy. (For example, his former lover and longtime friend Liz Sheridan continues to work, and will live on forever in syndication-land as Jerry's mother on *Seinfeld*.) And it's difficult to see, for example, how Rock Hudson's life and times would have been the least bit different had James Dean been in the world. No rational mind can find a cause-and-effect there. (Of course, no rational mind would embrace the concept of curses anyway.)

James Dean died in a relatively routine traffic fatality. All that has happened since then—the mushrooming of the legend, the marketing of his image, the deification in song and story, the talk of curses—is the product of hype and coincidence, nothing more.

Death of
the Marlboro Man

The Marlboro Man was one of the greatest salesmen of the 20th century. In countless magazine ads dating back to the mid-1950s and in a stream of television commercials in the 1960s, he was the man's man who rode the open plains on his trusty horse, rounding up the cattle as the Elmer Bernstein score from *The Magnificent Seven* swelled in the background. His craggy, lined face was ruggedly handsome; his hands rough and weather-beaten. When he took a break to reflect on a hard day's work and light up a cigarette, millions of TV viewers were swept up by the invitation to "Come to the where the flavor is...Come to Marlboro Country."

Even after cigarette ads were banned from the airwaves in 1972, the Marlboro Man kept on riding, in billboard ads and in magazines. Such was his influence on pop culture that when Don Johnson and Mickey Rourke teamed to play a couple of renegade bank robbers in a 1991 action-thriller, they had two instantly recognizable names: Harley Davidson and the Marlboro Man. This immediately conveyed the message that these guys were rebellious rogues who lived outside the boundaries of strait-laced society. Everyone knows Harleys and Marlboros are for cool guys! (At least that must have been the marketing intentions behind this forgettable thriller pairing two of the hammiest and most self-involved actors around.)

Of course, it was all propaganda. The Marlboro Man wasn't just a mere salesman, he was a modern-day merchant of death—a paid actor trading in on the American cowboy myth to hawk cigarettes, not just on TV but on billboards and in countless magazine ads. And when the Marlboro Man died of lung cancer, it was a tragic but poignant reminder that the product he was pitching all those years can kill you.

The Marlboro Man did die of cancer, didn't he?

Well, yes—and no. The legend of the Marlboro Man's death is a complicated blend of reality and misinformation, made all the more complicated by the agendas of a tobacco giant and some antismoking groups, and the fact that two Marlboro Men had similar-sounding last names.

Long before the Marlboro Man became a symbol of masculinity and individualism, Marlboros were introduced to the American public as cigarettes for women. Philip Morris debuted the brand in the 1920s with the slogan, "Mild as May," and magazine and newspaper ads featured a feminine hand reaching for a Marlboro. In the 1930s, the tips were colored red—the better to camouflage lipstick smears.

By the 1950s, with sales faltering, Philip Morris hired the Leo Burnett Company (creator of such commercial icons as the Jolly Green Giant, the Pillsbury Doughboy, Morris the Cat, the Keebler elves, and Tony the Tiger) to create a new, manly image for Marlboro cigarettes. The "Tattoed Man" campaign began in 1955 with a series of tough guys, such as pilots, sea captains, hunters, and cattle ranchers—all with tattoos of anchors on their wrists—touting Marlboros in print ad campaigns. The cowboy/rancher character was the most popular of the bunch, and in 1957, the Marlboro Man was born in a multipage ad in *Life* magazine, titled, "The Marlboro Man speaks for himself."

There were photos of the Marlboro Man in action, and a printed narrative: "I'm a rancher. Grew up in this part of the country...I like the life a man leads out here...[I] like to smoke, too. My brand's Marlboro...."

The Marlboro Man told us more about himself in subsequent print ads, but by the time he appeared on TV in 1963, he was such a familiar character that he didn't have to speak; he just had to ride and smoke, ride and smoke, as the music swelled and a narrator told us to "Come to where the flavor is...."

A number of models, actors, and real-life ranchers portrayed the Marlboro Man in the first print campaigns. Among them was David McLean, who also played the Marlboro Man when those TV ads started running in 1963. McLean, a native of Ohio, was never a "real" cowboy; after World War II, he moved to Los Angeles and pursued a career as a stage actor and a sketch artist, and he started finding regular work on TV by the late 1950s, eventually landing guest spots on nearly every Western series, including *Gunsmoke*, *Bonanza*, *High Chapparal*, *The Virginian,* and *The Westerner*. He even had a show of his own in 1960: *Tate*, a summer replacement for *The Perry Como Show*. *TV Guide* put McLean on its cover in June of 1960 and touted him as the next big cowboy star, but the show was a ratings failure, and McLean went back to the acting fringes, appearing in movies such as *Kingdom of the Spiders* with William Shatner and *Death Sport* with David Carradine—and in commercials for Marlboro.

It wasn't as if McLean was touting a product he didn't believe in. He had been a regular smoker since the age of 12, and his preferred brands were Marlboro and Chesterfield. According to McLean's family, he sometimes had to smoke as many as five packs a day when he was shooting ads for Marlboro, and Philip Morris continued to send him boxes of free smokes long after his association with the company had ended.

In 1985, McLean was diagnosed with emphysema, and in 1993 he underwent surgery to remove a tumor from his right lung. Two years later, McLean died of lung cancer at UCLA Medical Center in Westwood. He was 73.

McLean's family filed a wrongful death suit against Philip Morris, Inc., in 1996, seeking punitive and exemplary damages.

"Even the Marlboro Man was not immune from the effects of cigarette smoking," said Don Howarth, an attorney for the McLean family. "What is important about this case is that David McLean is the model of what the tobacco industry has done—hook smokers when they are young and then rely on the addictive qualities of their product to keep them enslaved."

Most of the rulings in the case have gone in favor of the defendants, but as of this writing, the lawsuit remains in play.

Another "Marlboro Man," Wayne McLaren, was a veteran smoker who died of lung cancer in July 1992, at the age of 51. Unlike McLean, who didn't make a public issue out of his illness, McLaren, in his last years, was a high-profile crusader against smoking. He toured schools to warn children about smoking, he appeared in a documentary called *The Tobacco Wars,* and he spoke before the Massachusetts legislature and the board of Philip Morris about the dangers of smoking.

Days before he succumbed, McLaren gave an interview from his hospital bed in which he said, "I've spent the last month of my life in an incubator and I'm telling you, it's just not worth it."

His mother, Louise McLaren, told the *Los Angeles Times*: "Some of his last words were: 'Take care of the children. Tobacco will kill you, and I am living proof of it.'"

McLaren also had much stronger cowboy credentials than McLean. He was on the professional rodeo circuit for about 10 years, and then found work as a stuntman and bit player in TV shows such as *Mission: Impossible* and *Gunsmoke*, and movies such as *Paint Your Wagon* and *Junior Bonner*. But he never veered from his cowboy ways of drinking and smoking (Kools was his preferred brand) and womanizing and getting into barroom scrapes.

To make ends meet, McLaren occasionally did print modeling—and one of those gigs was for Marlboro Texan Poker Cards, in which he appeared as one of five cowboys playing cards. McLaren's longtime companion, Ellen Brubaker, claimed McLaren also appeared in magazine print ads, but Philip Morris maintained that McLaren "was not a Marlboro Man."

If McLaren appeared in only the group ad for a Marlboro gift product, I'd have to side with the tobacco company on this one. And even if McLaren did a magazine ad, he was never the Marlboro Man at any time during the five-decade run of the campaign, certainly not of the magnitude of McLean, or of Bigun Bradley, a real cowboy who was the primary face of the Marlboro campaign for much of the mid- and late-1960s. (Bradley died under suspicious circumstances in 1973 when he and his horse were found drowned in a pond. Cause of death: two blows to the head.)

The lead Marlboro Man of the 1990s was Wyoming rancher Daryl Winfield — who became something of an urban (rural?) legend himself in 1993, when radio ads for the Great American Smokeout mentioned his name as one of the Marlboro Men who had died of smoking-related ailments. Apparently there had been some confusion stemming from the death of Montana native McLaren a year earlier.

As an icon, the Marlboro Man is not dead, though he's certainly not as pervasive as he was 35 years ago, when he was a dominant presence on TV, on the radio, in massive billboard campaigns, and in newspapers and magazines. In conjunction with the $206-billion agreement between the tobacco companies and the attorneys general for 46 states in 1998, almost all forms of outdoor tobacco advertising were to be phased out, reducing the Marlboro Man's workload to just newspapers, magazines, and direct-mail campaigns.

As for the oft-repeated statement, "The Marlboro Man died of lung cancer," it's both accurate and misleading. What's beyond dispute is that one of the men who made the Marlboro Man a star died of lung cancer, and another man who did at least one ad for Marlboro also succumbed to the disease.

And both men would have lived longer and healthier lives if they'd never taken up the deadly habit.

Dead
Legends

Mark Twain was arguably the most famous person in America in 1897, when he found himself having to refute stories about his demise with the famously wry comment: "Rumors of my death have been greatly exaggerated."

We've all heard that line dozens of times, and we've seen it invoked in stories about everything from the economy ("Reports of the death of the bull market have been greatly exaggerated") to sports ("Reports of the death of defense in the NFL have been greatly exaggerated") to politics ("Reports of the death of Al Gore's career have been greatly exaggerated"). It is one of the most familiar quotes in American lore.

There's only one problem, as we like to say here at Urban Legends Central: Twain never uttered those exact words.

In late spring of 1897, there indeed were reports that Twain, aka Samuel Clemens, had passed away while abroad. He cleared up the confusion with a cable from London that read:

> *James Ross Clemens, a cousin of mine, was seriously ill two or three weeks ago in London, but is well now. The report of my illness grew out of his illness, the report of my death an exaggeration.*
> —*Mark Twain.*

So he sort of said it, but he didn't actually say it. Gee, next we'll find out that James Cagney never said, "You dirty rat, you killed my brother!"; Cary Grant never said, "Judy, Judy, Judy!"; and Humphrey Bogart never uttered the exact phrase, "Play it again, Sam," in *Casablanca*.

Um, never mind.

Decades after Twain's actual passing in 1910, modern-day celebs such as Kirk Cameron, Adam Rich, and Scott Baio have found themselves in the unusual position of denying reports of their own deaths. (They've also found themselves in the unusual position of realizing their careers had peaked before they were of legal age, but that's another story for another time.) Let's separate the myth from the truth in this list of some of the most ubiquitous celebrity-death ULs of the last 30 years—including false rumors about deaths as well as misleading reports about the ways in which some celebrities who are dead actually died.

MYTH: Kirk Cameron of *Growing Pains* was killed in a bizarre bowling accident.

REALITY: Cameron is alive and well, having most recently appeared in the Christian movie *Left Behind* with his wife, Chelsea Noble (who once appeared on *Seinfeld* as a woman who was attracted to George because he looked like her boyfriend, "only taller and with more hair").

A few years ago, message boards on the Internet were hot with the rumor that a newspaper in Ridgewood, N.J., had reported that Kirk Cameron, best known for his role as Mike Seaver on *Growing Pains,* had died after slipping and hitting his head in a bowling alley.

An honorary staff member of the Urban Legends Research Team interviewed Cameron in January of 2001 and bravely asked him if he was aware of the bowling-death UL. The perplexed Cameron replied: "I never heard about that. It didn't happen. I'm right here."

Well, yes. We know that. My colleague had to go on to explain to Cameron what an urban legend is, as he expressed to her that he had never heard of the term. And even after she gave him a primer, he seemed confused by the whole thing.

MYTH: Paul McCartney died more than 30 years ago and was replaced by a female look-alike.

REALITY: Paul McCartney recently became the first musician to have a net worth of more than a billion dollars. If that ain't livin', I don't know what is.

MYTH: Roy of Siegfried and Roy is dead, and Roy's cousin has replaced Roy.

REALITY: This is kind of a tricky one as neither Siegfried nor Roy are actual human beings. They're animatronic figures, and as such are immortal and will never die.

Myth: Jerry "the Beaver" Mathers was killed in Vietnam.

Reality: Jerry "the Beaver" Mathers is a middle-aged man who keeps showing up in those *Still the Beaver* reunion TV movies. One of these days, we'll see him in *Grumpy Old Beaver*.

Myth: A stuntman died during the filming of *Ben-Hur*.

Reality: Despite persistent claims that the stunt double for Stephen Boyd was killed during the filming of the chariot race, and that director William Wyler left the scene in the final cut, there's no indication that anyone was killed or seriously injured during the making of the 1959 epic. The worst mishap on record was Charlton Heston's stunt double sustaining a gash to the chin that required a couple of stitches.

(Questions about the rumored death dominated a press junket for the film, prompting an assistant director to berate reporters and sarcastically claim that "20 men died" while making the movie.)

There's also no truth to the rumor that a stuntman lost his life during the making of *How the West Was Won*. However, a stuntman reportedly was killed during the making of the silent film titled *Ben-Hur*, which was made in the mid-1920s.

Myth: Shirley Eaton, the actress who played the evil villain's secretary, Jill Masterson, in *Goldfinger* who dies in the movie after being covered in gold paint, actually died in real life after her skin was unable to "breathe" through the paint.

Reality: Eaton walked away from the scene unharmed, and retired from acting a few years later at the age of 32. She has lived a mostly quiet life out of the spotlight since then, but in the fall of 2000 she made a surprise guest appearance at an English car dealership's anniversary party, where she told reporters, "I was only in *Goldfinger* for five minutes, but it made me internationally known—that just shows what a funny business it is."

MYTH: Adam Rich, the little moppet from *Eight Is Enough*, died in 1996.

REALITY: In 1996, a San Francisco-based satirical magazine called *Might* published a cover story titled, "Fare Thee Well, Gentle Friend." Inside was a lengthy article about the life and times of the late Adam Rich.

It was all a hoax, done with Rich's cooperation—but predictably, he found himself having to hit the publicity circuit to let people know that reports of his death had been, well, you know.

"If you can't laugh at yourself, you've missed the biggest f------ joke of your life," said Rich in a story published in *San Francisco Weekly*. "We collaborated on a very outrageous, outlandish, embellished story of my death. All too often, the media distorts and inflates, and tastelessly exploits celebrities' deaths to sell a magazine."

(Note: For a detailed account of the *Might* magazine hoax, pick up the Dave Eggers book *A Heartbreaking Work of Staggering Genius*.)

MYTH: Susan Olsen, who played Cindy on *The Brady Bunch*, died of a drug overdose.

REALITY: Olsen is fine—but the rumors probably started when another actress, Jennifer Runyon, portrayed Cindy in the 1988 TV movie *A Very Brady Christmas,* instead of Olsen. (Runyon's other memorable part was as the young woman with pyschic powers who charms Bill Murray in the opening scene of the first *Ghostbusters*.) The fact is that so many child stars have had rocky transitions to adulthood and anonymity, it's not hard to believe that yet another one hit the skids. At least two former child stars have died of drug overdoses: Dana Plato from *Diff'rent Strokes* died in 1999 at the age of 34; and Anissa Jones, who played Buffy on *Family Affair*, died in 1976 at the age of 18.

Myth: Before shooting her husband and herself, Phil Hartman's wife, Brynn, listened more than 50 times to the song "Ava Adore" from the Smashing Pumpkins' album *Adore*, with its aching, screeching chorus of "We must never be apart!"

Reality: The Hartman tragedy occurred on May 28, 1998. "Adore" was released in the United States in June of 1998.

Myth: George Reeves, who played Superman on the old TV series from the 1950s, committed suicide when he went insane and actually believed he would fly when he jumped out of a skyscraper window.

Reality: Sadly, Reeves did commit suicide—by shooting himself in the head in 1959 in the bedroom of his home while a party was taking place downstairs.

Myth: Brandon Lee was killed on the set of *The Crow* by a gang of Hong Kong mobsters after he refused to allow them to control his career.

Reality: Lee was killed when a dummy bullet (a real bullet without gun powder) was inadvertently left in the barrel of a gun to be used in a scene where he was shot. When the gun was fired, the blank propelled the dummy bullet into his midsection. And no, the scene was not left in the movie.

Myth: Rudolph Valentino died after eating food made with aluminum pots and pans.

Reality: In the 1920s, aluminum was erroneously cited by some quacks as the source of innumerable ailments. Valentino actually died from a perforated ulcer in 1926, at the age of 31.

And finally: The kid who played Mikey in the Life cereal commercials did not die from ingesting Pop Rocks candy and washing it down with soda pop. John Gilchrist is alive and well, though the UL about his explosive death has inspired an episode of *The Simpsons* as well as a scene in the movie *Urban Legends*.

And Finally...

Women Speak
in Estrogen...

For several years, *The Simpsons* creator Matt Groening has been credited as the author of one of the most widely circulated humor essays on the Internet. It's titled, "Women Speak in Estrogen and Men Listen in Testosterone," and it's about the fundamental differences between men and women.

For example:

SHOES: When preparing for work, a woman will put on a Mondi wool suit, then slip on Reebok sneakers. She will carry her dress shoes in a plastic bag from Saks. When a woman gets to work, she will put on her dress shoes. Five minutes later, she will kick them off because her feet are under the desk.

A man will wear the same pair of shoes all day.

You can find the article on hundreds of joke sites and in dozens of Internet chat rooms. Using the ever-valuable Google search engine, I typed in the keywords "Matt Groening" and "Testosterone," and found more than 170 sites containing the essay.

All attributing it to Groening.

Sections of the essay have been quoted in a number of newspapers. In November of 1999, the *Edmonton Journal* and the *Calgary Herald* had articles on the subject.

"How different are men and women? Here are four ways from writer/cartoonist Matt Groening in 'Women Speak in Estrogen, Men Listen in Testosterone':

"'A man has six items in his bathroom—toothbrush, toothpaste, shaving cream, razor, a bar of Dial soap, and a towel from the Holiday Inn. The average number of items in the typical woman's bathroom is 437. A man could not identify most of these items....'"

Groening's musings also appeared in one of those radio "joke sheets" that circulate through stations across the country. I remember hearing a duo in Chicago reading the article on the air in the late 1990s.

Only one problem with all of this: Groening didn't write it, nor has he ever claimed it as his own. (The genius who gave the world *The Simpsons* hardly needs to be taking credit for a mildly amusing article about the differences between boys and girls!) Groening has even disavowed the piece in interviews—but once something like this has been unleashed on the Internet, there's no stopping it. Not only has it been forwarded thousands of times, it's even been translated into several foreign languages. I'm surprised it's not a collection of bumper stickers by now.

TIME: When a woman says she'll be ready to go out in five minutes, she's using the same meaning of time as when a man says the football game will be over in five minutes.

OFFSPRING: A woman knows all about her children. She knows about dentist appointments and soccer games and romances and best friends and favorite foods and secret fears and hopes and dreams. A man is vaguely aware of some short people living in his house.

In 1997, the New York *Daily News* did a story about the essay, headlined, *"Simpsons* Guy No Net-Wit Wag":

"On a piece of e-mail that's been forwarded to thousands of Internet users, Groening is trumpeted as the author of 'Women Speak in Estrogen and Men Listen in Testosterone,' a humorous article comparing the sexes...

"'I didn't write it! I didn't write it!' Groening told the *Daily News*."

Groening goes on to call the article "mildly amusing" and admits he "laughed out loud" when he read the line: "Women love cats. Men say they love cats, but when women aren't looking, men kick cats."

The *Daily News* said the mix-up is "a near rerun of an episode...when Internet users started circulating a copy of a graduation speech that Kurt Vonnegut supposedly had delivered to MIT's class of 1997. The purported speech, though, was actually a newspaper article written by *Chicago Tribune* columnist Mary Schmich."

However, the New York *Daily News* was unable to ascertain the true author of the "Estrogen/Testosterone" piece. I'll do that in a moment.

Two years later, Groening told *Mother Jones* magazine, "One of the [drawbacks] of being successful is that stuff is out in my name that I didn't do. There's an essay floating all over the Internet on the difference between men and women. I did not write it."

Groening's denials notwithstanding, the legend continues to grow. In late 1999, a reporter for the *Augusta Chronicle* wrote, "Humorist Matt Groening defines the difference simply and succinctly: Women speak in estrogen and men listen in testosterone." And the essay continues to land in my mailbox.

Time now to solve this cyber-mystery. The original author of this essay is...

Me.

No kidding. I wrote the damn thing 15 years ago. The article appeared in my home paper, the *Chicago Sun-Times*, on May 11, 1986, under the headline, "It's time to face the facts: Men and women ARE different." In subsequent weeks, it was syndicated to a few other papers, including the *San Diego Union-Tribune*. How it leapt from the Internet Dark Ages of the mid-1980s to cyber-immortality—and, for that matter, how Groening's byline replaced mine atop an essay that otherwise has been reprinted verbatim—is beyond me. Somebody somewhere probably made an innocent cut-and-paste mistake, and the error was multiplied a thousandfold over the course of several years. D'oh!

As of this writing, the truth has been striking at least a small dent in this urban legend. A few newspapers are now attributing the infamous piece to yours truly, and I've seen some Internet Web sites that have restored authorship to the correct writer.

Not that I'm getting royalties or anything.

After years of chronicling urban legends involving other people, I now have a firsthand feeling of what it's like to be trapped in a web of misinformation. It's a little frustrating to see my work attributed to someone else—even if there's an implied compliment that people would believe that such a creative force as Groening could have written the piece.

Besides, it's not as if I'm being linked with a gerbil.

Bibliography and Notes

Back to *The Fugitive*

1. Associated Press. "Fugitive case to continue." 7 November 2000.

2. APBnews.com. "The Sheppard murder." FBI documents on file.

3. Kuznik, Frank. "Terrible burden." *New Times*, 20 April 2000, Features section.

4. Renzhofer, Martin. "Like a western hero, *Fugitive* wanders through, falls in love, rights wrongs." *The Salt Lake Tribune*, 12 October 2000.

5. Galbraith, Jane. "Son of Sam? Not *Fugitive*, creator says." *Chicago Sun-Times*, 19 September 1993, Showcase section, 2.

6. King, Susan. "Let the chase begin (Again) with New *Fugitive* series." *Los Angeles Times*, 29 August 2000, Calendar section, 1.

7. Clifford, Terry. "Tracking down the show 30 years later." *Chicago Tribune*, 1 August 1993, Arts section, 5.

8. Simonich, Milan. "*Fugitive* creator rejects claims." *The Orange County Register*, 27 February 2000, A33.

9. Smith, Stacy Jenel. "*The Fugitive* is based on Sam Sheppard case." *Chattanooga Times*, 1 August 2000, Lifestyle section, E4.

10. CourtTV online. "Sam Sheppard estate lays out its version of 1954 case in pretrial statement."

11. Interview, Sam Reese Sheppard, January, 2001.

12. Press conference in Los Angeles for *The Fugitive*, July, 2000.

"And the Password Is..."

1. Farr, Jamie. *Just Farr Fun*. Eubanks/Donizetti, Inc., 1994.

2. Wolff, Alexander. "Bo on the go." *Sports Illustrated*, 5 September 1984, 154.

Touched By an Atheist

1. Gesalman, Anne Belli. "An atheist's last rites." *Newsweek*, 12 February 2001, 27.

2. Statement from FCC.

Myths of the Super Bowl

1. Perry, Tony. "Myth America: the legend of Super Sunday." *Los Angeles Times*, 31 January 1999, 1.

2. Associated Press. "Sub-par TV ratings for game." 30 January 2001.

3. Kicklighter, Kirk. "Super Bowl myths debunked." *Atlanta Journal and Constitution*, 28 January 2001, 1A.

4. Wilkinson, Jack. "Reporter wants to put end to modern-day urban legend." *Atlanta Journal and Constitution*, Sports section, 25 January 2000, 3H.

5. Adams, Cecil. "Does violence against women rise 40 percent during the Super Bowl?" The Straight Dope column, 14 April 2000.

6. Clark, Jayne. "Super Bowl hits and myths." *USA Today*, 26 January 2001.

"Willy Gilligan" and the Seven Deadly Sins

1. Schwartz, Sherwood. *Inside Gilligan's Island*. New York: St. Martin's Press, 1994.

2. Denver, Bob. *Gilligan, Maynard and Me*. Secaucus, N.J.: Carol Publishing Group, 1993.

3. Morton, Brian. "L'isle de Gilligan." *Lingua franca*, December, 1990, 28.

4. Dumas, Alan. "Here on *Gilligan's Island*. Creator recalls his days on immensely popular television sitcom." *Denver Rocky Mountain News*, 29 September 1994, 15D.

5. Ahrens, Frank. "Just sit right back and you'll hear a tale." *The Washington Post*, 21 October 1998, Style section, D01.

Cosby Buys *The Little Rascals*

1. Maltin, Leonard, and Richard W. Bann. *The Little Rascals: The Life and Times of Our Gang*. New York: Random House, Inc., 1992.

2. Feran, Tom. "Rascals were beloved in their time." *Cleveland Plain Dealer*, 13 December 1992, H9.

3. Ramsey, Steve. *The Little Rascals* Web site: *www.ramseyltd.com/rascals/*

Bert and Ernie Are Gay and Dead!

1. Conklin, Mike. "A *Wonderful* moment: the stories behind the faces of the movie's poignant scene." *Chicago Tribune*, 21 December 2000, Tempo section, 5.

2. Caroll, Jon. "A few tiny errors." *San Francisco Chronicle*, 3 January 2000, D8.

3. Weale, Natasha. "20 useless things you probably don't want to know." *Scottish Daily Record*, 20 February 1999, 43.

4. "Are *Sesame*'s Bert and Ernie named after movie characters?" *Minneapolis Star-Tribune*, 2 February 1997.

5. Garrett, Craig. "It's a wonderful—and debated—*Life*: after 50 years, Capra's classic still touches us in unique ways." *The Detroit News*, 11 December 1996.

6. Cox News Service. "What do you know of *Life*?", 15 December 1992.

7. Anderson, Kurt. *The Real Thing*. 1980.

8. E-mail correspondence with Kurt Anderson, January, 2001.

9. Hermman, Brenda. "Have you heard? Ernie's dead!" *Chicago Tribune*, 10 November 1992, C1.

10. "Just as alive as he ever was." *Louisville Courier-Journal*, 1 March 1993, 2A.

11. Stroup, Sheila. "Goofy, yes, but not gay." *The New Orleans Times-Picayune*, 2 November 1993, B1.

12. Reimer, Susan. "Believe this: muppet Bert isn't dead, isn't dying." *The Baltimore Sun*, 7 December 1997, 1J.

The Newlywed Game **Blooper**

1. *The Newlywed Game* clip at: *www.hitplay.com*, via Game Show Network.

2. Fretts, Bruce. "Laughing all the way to the Eubanks." *Entertainment Weekly*, 12 December 1997, 65.

3. Keeps, David A. "She is...Pamela Anderson." *Playboy*, February, 1999, 124.

4. *The Newlywed Game* tape from 11 august 1977, courtesy of Game Show Network.

Bogart the Gerber Baby?

1. McCarthy, Clifford, and Lauren Bacall. *The Complete Films of Humphrey Bogart*. Secaucus, N.J.: Carol Publishing Group, 1985.

2. Sperber, A.M., and Eric Lax. *Bogart*. New York: William Morrow, 1998.

3. Meyers, Jeffrey. *Bogart: A Life in Hollywood*. New York: Fromm International Publishing Corporation, 1999.

4. Gerber Web site: *www.gerber.com*

5. Rosenberg, Mike. "Tribute to Humphrey Bogart" Web site: *www.macconsult.com/bogart/*

6. Collister, Mary. "She had the cutest little Gerber face." *St. Petersburg Times*, 29 July 1992.

7. Evertz, Mary. "The face behind the Gerber baby." *St. Petersburg Times*, 14 March 1997, D1.

8. Interview with Ann Turner Cook, February, 2001.

Did the Duke Dodge the Draft?

1. Adler, Renata. "*Green Berets* as viewed by John Wayne." *The New York Times*, 20 June 1968.

2. Adams, Cecil. "Was John Wayne a draft dodger?" *The Straight Dope* column, 10 July 1998.

3. Wills, Garry. *John Wayne's America: The Politics of Celebrity*. New York: Simon & Schuster, 1997.

4. Olson, James S., and Randy Roberts. *John Wayne: American*. New York: Free Press, 1995.

5. Connors, Martin and Jim Graddock. *VideoHound's Golden Movie Retriever 2000*. Michigan: Visible Ink Press, 2000.

6. Hainer, Cathy. "Back in the bloom of health." *USA Today*, 11 January 1999, D1.

7. Horiuchi, Vince. "Net nonsense: medical Internet legends are enough to scare the antibodies right out of you." *The Salt Lake Tribune*, 10 February 2000, C1.

8. Stenn, David. *Clara Bow Running Wild*. New York: Doubleday, 1988.

Cher's Rib Removal

1. Stoppard, Miriam. "I'm in a mess over bats in the belfry." *London Daily Mirror*, 3 November 2000, 39.

2. Pearlman, Cindy. "Putting the rumors to rest." *Chicago Sun-Times*, 21 April 2000, 45.

3. Patterson, Rod and the *Oregonian* staff. "Why does he call himself Fluffy?" *The Portland Oregonian*, 10 February 2000, E02.

4. Moir, Jan. "I'm closer than ever to Sonny." *London Daily Telegraph*, 4 January 1999, 13.

5. Smith, Andy. "Cher's resilience goes deeper than silicone." *Providence Journal-Bulletin*, 15 July 1999, 5L.
6. Dunn, Jancee. "Tori tells." *Harper's Bazaar*, August, 1999, 30.

Hanoi Jane Fonda

1. Abrams, Garry. "Fonda meets with vets, wins a few hearts," *Los Angeles Times*, 20 June 1988, E-1.
2. Kevin Markey and *Ladies Home Journal. The 100 Most Important Women of the Century*. Meredith Books, 1998.
3. Emery, David. "Hanoi Jane rumors blend fact and fiction." *about.com*, Urban Legends and Folklore Web site, 3 November 1999.
4. Boule, Margie. "An errant Jane Fonda story and other false e-mails of modern myth-making." *The Portland Oregonian*, 19 September 2000, C01.
5. Anderson, Christopher. *Citizen Jane: The Turbulent Life of Jane Fonda*. Henry Holt, 1990.
6. "Barbara Walters salutes a century of great women." *Chattanooga Times*, 30 April 1999.
7. Interview with Ann Mills Griffiths, executive director of the National League of POW/MIA Families, January, 2001.
8. Interview with Capt. Mike McGrath, USN-Ret., January, 2001.

Fargo-ing the Truth

1. Karger, Dave. "Joel Coen: a statue might lie hidden under the deadly snowdrifts of *Fargo*." *Entertainment Weekly*, March 1997, 112.
2. Alesia, Tom. "*Fargo* plays with the truth." *Madison* (Wis.) *Capital Times*, 5 April 1996, 1D.
3. Vognar, Chris. "Is Coens' *Fargo* true lies?" *Dallas Morning News*, 5 October 1996, 5C.
4. "Does *Fargo* forego the facts?" *Minneapolis Star-Tribune*, 8 March 1996.
5. Boyar, Jay. "*Fargo* tells crime tale that is odd, fascinating." *The Orlando Sentinel*, 22 March 1996, Calendar section, 17.
6. Covert, Colin. "*Fargo* events never happened, BCA says." *Minneapolis Star-Tribune*, 3 March 1996.
7. Havis, Richard James. "Real life, through a filter strangely." *South China Morning Post*, 22 September 1996, 4.

Johnny Rocco's Recount

1. Saunders, Michael and Jim Sullivan. Names & Faces column, *The Boston Globe*, 8 December 2000, F4.

2. "News Bazaar: Largo the key to this election?" *The Hotline*, People section, 8 December 2000.
3. Ayres, B. Drummond. "Edward G. Robinson on Florida politics." *The New York Times*, 10 December 2000, Section 1, 51.

I'm Drunk and You're a Prostitute
1. Interview with Chris White, January, 2001.
2. TopFive Web site: *www.topfive.com*
3. Seelye, Katharine. "Unwitting authors find Gore got their jokes." *The New York Times*, 15 May 2000.
4. Lipper, Hal. "Will *Mr. Cat Poop* clean up at the box office in Hong Kong? *The Wall Street Journal*, 13 April 1998.
5. Sterngold, James. "Lost, and gained, in the translation." *The New York Times*, Week in Review section, 14 November 1998.
6. Barnhart, Aaron. "ABC is the latest to fall for spoof." *Kansas City Star*, 7 January 1999, E7.
7. "Movie titles take a humorous turn." *Atlanta Journal and Constitution.* 28 April 1998, 9C.
8. Jennings, Peter. "*ABC World News Tonight*." 5 January 1999.
9. Parsons, Charlotte. "What about *Dumb and Dumber*?" *South China Morning Post*, 17 June 2000, 16.

The Jesus Chronicles
1. Rich, Frank. "'Corpus Christi' D.O.A." *The New York Times*, 17 October 1998, Section A, 15.
2. Leo, John. "Bigotry still has no place in work of art." *Detroit News*, 9 June 1998, A7.
3. Applebome, Peter. "In reversal, theater vows to stage play that drew threats." *The New York Times*, 29 May 1998, Section A, 1.
4. Armbrust, Roger. "Panning anti-Catholic art." *Back Stage*, 17 March 2000, 5.

Casa-bunka
1. Associated Press. "Behind the scenes of *Casablanca*." 5 June 1992.
2. Haskell, Molly. "The love that's forever: making matches." *The New York Times*, 23 May 1999, Section 2, 1.
3. Meyer, Norma. "Brando as Lawrence? Book finds missed castings." *The San Diego Union-Tribune*, 24 April 1994, E6.
4. Guttridge, Peter. "What if...Ronald Reagan had smoldered in *Casablanca*?" *London Independent*, 18 January 1996, Film section, 7.

5. Goldman, Steven. "Here's looking at you, Ronald." *London Times*, 20 December 1998, Features section.

6. Arnold, Gary. "Casting choices: pick the players for the part, and change film history." *The Washington Post*, 21 September 1980, L-4.

7. Davis, Ivor. "The parts they didn't play." *Montreal Gazette*, 24 April 1994, F1.

8. Purgavie, Dermot. "You must remember this." *London Daily Mail*, 6 July 1992.

The Curse of *Poltergeist*

1. Cieply, Michael. "*Poltergeist III*: the dilemma." *Los Angeles Times*, 21 March 1988, Calendar Section, 1.

2. Burr, Ty. "Was *Poltergeist* cursed?" *Entertainment Weekly*, 31 January 1997, 72.

3. Salem, Rob. "Superstitious 'hogwash' irks *Poltergeist* actress." *Toronto Star*, 20 June 1988, C4.

Monica Puts Foot in Mouth

1. *Larry King Live*. CNN transcript, 3 January 2000.

2. Pandora. *The London Independent*, 21 January 2000, 4.

3. Flick, Bill. "AUGGGHH! In death, he's just like Charlie Brown's life." *Bloomington Daily Pantagraph*, 18 February 2000, A16.

4. Borsellino, Rob. "Examples of political incompetence always abound." *Des Moines Register*, 5 February 2000, Metro section, 1.

5. Whitaker, James. "James Whitaker Column." *London Daily Mirror*, 26 February 2000, 33.

6. Patterson, Rod and *Oregonian* staff. "Elvis' little girl prepares to take third aisle walk with a young singer-songwriter from Hawaii." *The Portland Oregonian*, 2 February 2000, D02.

Johnny Carson's Quips

1. Atkinson, Terry. "Tracking a vanishing video trove." *Los Angeles Times*, 29 August 1986, Calendar section, 21.

2. Cox, Stephen. *Here's Johnny*. New York: Harmony Books, 1992.

3. Gabor, Zsa Zsa. *One Lifetime is Not Enough*. New York: Delacorte Press, 1991.

4. Mitchell, Sean. "TV Confidential." *TV Guide*, 25 July 1998, 13.

"Lido Deck, Sir?"

1. Cawley, Janet. "Sailing the congressional seas: Fred Grandy goes to Washington, but Gopher stays home." *Chicago Tribune*, 20 March 1987, Tempo section, 1.

2. Bolton, Alexander, et al. "*Love Boat* myth: former Rep. Fred Grandy fesses up." *The Hill*, 13 September 2000, 9.

3. Elvin, John. "Inside the Beltway." *Washington Times*, 21 May 1990, A6.

4. Rubin, Neal. "Pages get an insider's view of the workings of Congress." *Orange County Register*, 5 July 1992, G02.

5. VandeHei, Jim. "Heard on the Hill." *Roll Call*, 6 August 1998.

6. Rahner, Mark. "Over coffee with Fred Grandy." *The Seattle Times*, 19 June 2000, F1.

7. Allis, Tim. "Sea change." *People* magazine, 16 February 1987, 102.

Unrelated Legends

1. Shull, R.K. "Squelch that one: Susan Lucci isn't Phyllis Diller's daughter." *The Indianapolis Star*, 24 October 2000, E07.

2. Williams, Jeannie. "Is Lucci linked to that Diller dame?" *USA Today*, 14 January 2000, 4E.

3. Hirsch, Lynda. "No! Diller isn't Lucci's real-life mother." *Fort Lauderdale Sun-Sentinel*, 27 March 1993, 4D.

4. Fenner, Pat. "Soap star Susan Lucci isn't one of Phyllis Diller's children." *St. Petersburg Times*, 4 March 1987, 2.

5. Official biography pages, network press releases, Internet fan sites for: Phyllis Diller, Susan Lucci, Robin Strasser, Neil Diamond, Dustin Diamond, and the Beastie Boys.

Was Lucy a Commie?

1. FBI file on Lucille Ball.

2. "Lucille Ball probe finds no evidence of Red Party ties." *Los Angeles Herald Examiner*, 12 September 1953.

3. "Stars name on Red slate." *Los Angeles Herald Examiner*, 12 September 1953.

4. Sanders, Coyne Steven, and Tom Gilbert. *Desilu: The Story of Lucille Ball and Desi Arnaz*. New York: William Morrow, 1993.

5. Hopper, Hedda. "Happy to have cleared up rumors, Lucy tells columnist Hedda Hopper." *Los Angeles Times*, 12 September 1953.

Mean Martha Stewart

1. Roche, B.J. "Peaks and valleys; would you believe?" *The Boston Globe*, 3 September 2000, C1.

2. Gearty, Robert. "Mean Martha: East Hampton neighbors fight a border war." *New York Daily News*, 8 June 1997, 8.

3. Oppenheimer, Jerry. *Just Desserts*. New York: William Morrow, 1997.

Madonna, Tip-Top Starlet

1. Trudeau, Garry. "I am a tip-top starlet; in which something is lost, but much is gained, in the translation." *Time*, 20 May 1996, 84.
2. Thomas, Karen. "Madonna's Hungarian accent is on baby, men." *USA Today*, 2 May 1996, Life section, 2D.
3. Buchanan, Jim. "A failure to communicate can be good, old-fashioned fun." *Asheville Citizen-Times*, 25 May 1996, B1.
4. "Hungarian interviewers match wits with Madonna." *Charlotte News-Observer,* 16 May 1996, A2.
5. Levins, Harry. *St. Louis-Post Dispatch*, 17 May 1996, "People" Column, 2A.
6. Norman, Matthew. "Diary." *London Guardian*, 21 May 1996, 17.
7. "My, my, what the bold hussy-woman will say!" *Fort-Worth Star Telegram*. 20 May 1996, Life & Arts section, 2.
8. "Rock and Pop." *London Evening Standard,* 14 August 1998, 29.
9. O'Boyle, Jane. *Free Drinks For Ladies With Nuts: Delightfully Mangled English From Around the World*. New York: Dutton/Plume, 2000.

Let It Bleed

1. Swenson, John. "It's only rock and roll." UPI Arts & Entertainment, 6 September 2000.
2. Bledsoe, Wayne. "The Rolling Stones: start them up, they don't stop." *Knoxville News-Sentinel*, 24 October 1997, T8.
3. Bowie, Angela. *Backstage Passes: Life on the wild side with David Bowie.* Cooper Square Press, 2000.
4. Harrington, Richard. "The Stones, rough cut and satisfied." *The Washington Post*, 10 November 1983, C1.

It's Not Easy Being a Green CD

1. Schwartz, Bruce. "Felt-tip markers stir a hue and cry over CD clarity." *USA Today*, 10 May 1990, Life section.
2. Fantel, Hans. "Brush aside the idea of painting CD's." *The New York Times*, 3 June 1990, Section 2, 26.
3. Hunt, Kevin. "Nothing beats the sound of vinyl." *Hartford Courant*, 21 January 1995, 7C.
4. Parker, Dana J. "The green flash and other urban legends." *EMedia Magazine*, 1 September 2000, 72.
5. Considine, J.D. "The greening of America, CD style." *The Baltimore Sun*, April, 1990.

Eminem Lives!

1. Guzman, Isaac. "Hoax-hoax: netzoids had Eminem, Ulrich dead." *New York Daily News*, 21 December 2000, 48.
2. Strauss, Neil. "Seeking truth about Eminem." *The New York Times*, 21 December 2000, Section E, 3.
3. Emery, David. about.com's Urban Legends Web site.
4. Teenan, Tim. "The test." *London Times*, 28 December 2000, Features section.
5. Eminem Web site: *www.eminem.com*

"Fire and Rain"

1. Halperin, Ian. *Fire and Rain: the James Taylor Story*. Secaucus, N.J.: Citadel Press, 2000.
2. *Rolling Stone*, 18 February 1971.

Blondie Blunts Bundy?

1. Aparicio, Nester. "Encounter with a killer? Rock singer Deborah Harry tells of a scary ride with Ted Bundy." *St. Petersburg Times*, 8 November 1989, 3A.
2. Rule, Ann. *The Stranger Beside Me, 20th Anniversary Edition*. W.W. Norton and Co., 2000.
3. Associated Press. "Horror lives on a decade after Bundy's execution." 13 February 1999.
4. Associated Press. "Ted Bundy timeline." 13 February 1999.

Mama Cass and the Ham Sandwich

1. Guinn, Jeff. "Death can be the end of a good reputation." *Fort Worth Star-Telegram*, 15 May 1999, Life & Arts section, 1.
2. Reid, Melanie. "Death of a rock rebel." *Scottish Daily Record*, 23 November 1997, 4.
3. Moskowitz, Seth W. "A local art show with real taste." *The Washington Post*, 14 September 1978, DC2.
4. Marshall, Andrew. "No one's getting fat except Mama Cass." *London Guardian*, 26 July 1999, Features section, 6.
5. Vivinetto, Gina. "Immortal rockers and how they got that way." *St. Petersburg Times*, 21 January 2000, 19W.
6. Powell, Joanna. "Mama Cass choking rumor untrue." *Entertainment Weekly*, 4 August 1992, C-4.
7. McDonald, William. "A rock music 'Papa' finds calmer water as a children's host." *The New York Times*, Section 2, 33.

8. Phillips, John. *Papa John: the Autobiography of John Phillips*. Doubleday and Co., 1986.
9. Interview with Owen Elliott, February, 2001.

Death of the Marlboro Man
1. Marchese, John. "A rough ride." *The New York Times*, 13 September 1992, Section 9, 1.
2. McKeever, Lauren. "Wyoming Marlboro Man surprised to find out he's dead." *Idaho Falls Post Register*, 25 November 1993, A1.
3. Business Wire. "The original Marlboro Man dies from lung cancer caused by smoking; family sues tobacco companies for fraud and deceit." 19 September 1996.
4. Rooney, David. "Obituaries: David McLean." *Daily Variety*, 18 October 1995.
5. Johnson, Kevin. "Lung cancer ends life of former Marlboro Man." *Los Angeles Times*, 23 July 1992, Metro section, 6.
6. O'Connor, Clint. "Marlboro Man is ridin' hard out of town." *The San Diego Union-Tribune*, 19 March 999, E-3.
7. "Choice of Law: McLean v. Philip Morris Inc." *Tobacco Industry Litigation Reporter*, Vol. 15, No. 17, 11 August 2000, 6.
8. Price, Sean. "The war on tobacco." *The New York Times Upfront*, 20 September 1999, 13.

Dead Legends
1. Interview with Kirk Cameron, January, 2001.
2. Bentley, Rick. "Childish ways..." *Fresno Bee*, 1 September 2000, E.
3. "Best rumors of the century." *Toronto Star*. 31 December 1999, Entertainment section.
4. "Golden girl Shirley is star of show at Helston garages celebrations." *Plymouth Western Morning News*. 17 October 2000, 5.
5. Day, Crosby. "Gilt-edged James Bond." *The Orlando Sentinel*, 31 May 1992, 49.
6. Boulware, Jack. "The resurrection of Adam Rich." *San Francisco Weekly*, 8 May 1996.
7. Friedman, David R. "The mysterious legacy of Brandon Lee." *Today's Chiropractic*, May/June, 1996, 34-38.

Women Speak in Estrogen...
1. Mannes, George. "*Simpsons'* guy no net-wit wag." *New York Daily News*, 12 October 1997, 4.
2. Editorial (no byline), "Vive la difference." *Augusta Chronicle*, 1 December 2000, A04.

3. "How different are the sexes?" *Edmonton Journal*, 5 November 1999, L9.

4. Rosental, Laurie. "Behind the door: the differences between men and women," *Nation*, 18 May 1998.

NOTE: There are a number of helpful Web sites on urban legends. Two in particular offer outstanding analysis and research on ULs. They are:

1. The San Fernando Valley Folklore Society's Urban Legend Reference Page *www.snopes.com*

2. David Emery's about.com's urban legend page: *urbanlegends.about.com*

Index

Albert, Eddie, 43-44
Allen, Harley, 191-195
Arnaz, Desi, 151-157

Bacall, Lauren, 68, 106
Baio, Scott, 21-23, 215, 228
Ball, Lucille, 151-157
Barrymore, Drew, 129-130, 133
Beck, Julian, 124-125
Ben-Hur, 31, 230
Bergman, Ingrid, 120
Blue's Clues, 212-215
Bogart, Humphrey, 68-72, 106, 120, 228
Bond, Ward, 49
Brady Bunch, The, 231-232
Bundy, Ted, 196-199
Burns, Steve, 212-215

Cameron, Kirk, 228-229
Carson, Johnny, 138-142

Casablanca, 71, 72, 120-122, 228
Cass, Mama, 10, 207-211
CDs, greening of, 178-182
celebrities, related, 146-150
celebrity death legends, 227-233
Cher, 80-83
Clinton, Bill, 134, 135, 137
Cohen brothers, 95, 96
Cook, Ann Turner, 70-71
Cooper, Alice, 175-176
Corpus Christi, 117-118
Cosby, Bill, 45-47

Damone, Vic, 220
Dean, James, curse of, 216-220
Denver, Bob, 42, 130
Diamond, Neil, 149-150
Diller, Phyllis, 148-149
Dunne, Dominique, 123-125

Eaton, Shirley, 230-231
election recount, 104-107
Elliot, Mama Cass, 10, 207-211
Eminem, 183-186
Eubanks, Bob, 54-59

Faithful, Marianne, 175
Fargo, 95-98
Farr, Jamie, 25-26
Faylen, Frank, 49
"Fire and Rain," 187-190
Fonda, Jane, 66, 84-88
Fugitive, The, 13-20, 41

Gable, Clark, 76
Gabor, Eva, 43-44
Gabor, Zsa Zsa, 139-142
Gates, Bill, 165
Gerber, and Bogart, 69-71
Gere, Richard, 133
Gibson, Mel, 63-67
Gilchrist, John, 233
Gilligan's Island, 39-42, 45
Gone With the Wind, 120
Gore, Al, 66, 112
Grandy, Fred, 143-145
Green Acres, 43-44
Green, Tom, 10, 129-133
Groening, Matt, 237-240
Gunsmoke, 77-78

Harry, Deborah, 196-199
Hartman, Phil, 232
Harvey, Paul, 63-67
Henson, Jim, 49-50
Huggins, Roy, 17-18, 20

I Love Lucy, 152-157
It's a Wonderful Life, 48-52

Jagger, Mick, 175
"Jesus movie," 113-118
Joanie Loves Chachi, 21-23
John, Elton, 175
Jones, Anissa, 232

Key Largo, 105-107
Kiss Me Deadly, 102

Larry King Live, 134-137
Lee, Brandon, 232-233
Leno, Jay, 65, 80, 139
Letterman, David, 22, 65, 139
Lewinsky, Monica, 134-137
"Little Girl, The," 191-195
Little Rascals, The, 45-47
Louise, Tina, 39
Love Boat, The, 143
Lucci, Susan, 148-149

Madonna, 169-173
Mamas and The Papas, The, 207
Man Without a Face, The, 65-67
Manson, Marilyn, 81, 176
Marlboro Man, the, 221-226
Marx Brothers, 72
Marx, Groucho, 120
Mathers, Jerry, 230
McCartney, Paul, 229
McLaren, Wayne, 224-225
McLean, David, 223-226
McNally, Terrance, 117-118
Monroe, Marilyn, 89-92, 218

Montgomery, John Michael, 191-195
movie titles, translated, 108-112

Newlywed Game, The, blooper, 10, 25, 54-59
Night in Casablanca, A, 72
Nostradamus, 104-105, 107

O'Hair, Madalyn Murray, 28-31
O'Rourke, Heather, 123-125
Olsen, Susan, 231-232
Osbourne, Ozzy, 176

Password, 24-27
Peter, Paul & Mary, 200-204
Philip Morris, 222-223
Plato, Dana, 232
Poltergeist, curse of, 123-125
Presley, Elvis, 78
"Puff the Magic Dragon," 10, 200-204
Pulp Fiction, 99-103

Reagan, Ronald, 71, 120-122
Reeves, George, 232
Reynolds, Burt, 141-142
Rich, Adam, 10, 228, 231
Richards, Keith, 176-177
Rickles, Don, 163-165
Roach, Hal, 45-47
Robertson, Ed, 18
Robins, Oliver, 123
Robinson, Edward G., 105-107
Russell, Nipsey, 26

Sampson, Will, 124-125
Schwartz, Sherwood, 40-42
Sesame Street, 48-52
Sheppard, Dr. Sam, 14-20
Sheppard, Sam Reese, 16, 18
Sheridan, Ann, 120-122
Siegfried and Roy, 229
Sinatra, Frank, 163-164
Stewart, Martha, 158-161
Stewart, Rod, 175
Strasser, Robin, 148-149
Super Bowl, myths of the, 32-38
Super Password, 26

Tarantino, Quentin, 99-103
Taylor, James, 187-190
Tharp, Michelle Sue, 194-195
Tonight Show, The, 80, 138-142, 163
Touched by an Angel, 29-31
Twain, Mark, 227-228
$25,000 Pyramid, 24, 26

Valentino, Rudolph, 233

Wallis, Hal, 121-122
Walters, Barbara, 84-86, 88
Warner Bros., 68-72, 120-121
Wayne, John, 73-79
Williams, Doug, 37-38
Winfield, Daryl, 225
"Women Speak in Estrogen, Men Listen in Testosterone," 237-240

Zappa, Frank, 175
Ziffel, Arnold, 43-44

About
the Author

Richard Roeper is the co-host of the nationally syndicated *Ebert & Roeper and the Movies*. Roeper also writes a daily general interest column for the *Chicago Sun-Times*, which is distributed nationally by the New York Times Syndicate. He has won two Chicago/Midwest Emmys for his television commentaries on the Fox affiliate in Chicago, and he has hosted radio programs on a number of Chicago stations. The author lives in Chicago.